# 1000
## new eco designs
## and where to find them

**Rebecca Proctor**

Laurence King Publishing

1000
ne          gns

Published in 2009 by
Laurence King Publishing Ltd
361–373 City Road, London EC1V 1LR
United Kingdom
T +44 20 7841 6900
F +44 20 7841 6910
enquiries@laurenceking.com
www.laurenceking.com

A catalogue record for this book is available from
the British Library.

ISBN: 978 1 85669 585 5

Senior Editor: Gaynor Sermon
Copy Editor: Liz Dalby
Design: Peter Richardson
Picture Research: Fredrika Lökholm

Front cover (from top row, left to right):
Flytip Furniture, Alexena Cayless; Equus, Osian
Batyka Williams; Coatstand, David Sutton; Palette
chair, Nina Tolstrup; MH024 Storage, Matthew
Hilton; 3 Blocks, Kalon Studios; Flat Pack Table,
Freshwest; Shadey lamp, WIS Design; Manu
Windsor Chair, Mabeo; Natural Utensils, Bambu.

Back cover (from top row, left to right):
Frida lamp, Amy Adams; Candleholder, Stephen
Bretland; Colombo chair, Matthew Hilton; Bottle
Bulb light, Kessels Granger; YBA table, Peter
Masters; Salvation Stacks, Boym Partners;
Atomium lamp, Kundalini; Hanging Back,
Sebastien Hejna.

Printed in China

Author's dedication: For Sparkles in Trees

LAURENCE KING

# Contents

# Introduction

There's no doubt that the way we live is unsustainable. Mass dependence on fossil fuels has resulted in global warming and, despite growing awareness of the environmental consequences, our energy consumption is still soaring rapidly. The UK alone produces 220 million tonnes of waste per year, yet we still only reuse or recycle a fraction of this: the rest ends up as landfill. To make matters worse, in the last century this destructive activity has not just harmed our own environment but has also affected wildlife habitats, causing devastating losses to many animal species.

The word 'eco' has lately become something of a buzzword but, whatever the prevailing trend, there is no doubt that ecologically sensitive design has to become a permanent part of our lives. There is simply no other way.

Under the recent media onslaught of TV programmes and articles about food, we have all been taught to consider where the food on our plate comes from. Is your food local? Organic? Free range? Which farm did your potatoes come from? Were your strawberries shipped or air freighted, or grown nearby? Did the chicken you just ate lead a happy life? These are all questions we have been encouraged to ask ourselves – and rightly so – but how many of us stop to think about where the bed we sleep in every night came from? Who made it? What part of the world was it made in? What is it made from? And what effect did building the bed have on our environment?

While an obvious solution to the problems caused by over consumption would be to cease industrial production and never buy anything again, we would be denying ourselves one of the most basic human instincts, that of designing and making, and of enjoying the beauty of good design. It is also an impractical solution, considering the amount of jobs from industry that would be lost.

Throughout our lives it is realistic to expect that we are going to continue to consume, so this book allows you to shop responsibly by giving you 1000 inspiring and ethical choices of furniture and homewares. It's important to remember that, while the book may provide you with ideas, before you rush out and buy a table, ask yourself whether you really need it? If the answer is yes, buy a table with a design you love, in the best quality ethically sourced sustainable materials you can afford, and keep it for a lifetime. One good quality item will always bring you more pleasure and affect the environment far less than several substandard ones. It is a tragedy to see perfectly good furniture being discarded with the rubbish. It is even more frustrating to see people spending their hard-earned money on badly designed, poorly made, unethically produced 'value' furniture that will inevitably reach the landfill in a few years when the owners have tired of it or it has fallen to pieces.

Before the industrial revolution, when furniture and household goods were produced locally by blacksmiths, woodworkers and weavers, these skilled craftsmen used readily available local resources and made goods intended to last at least one lifetime. Unfortunately, since those days, mass produced manufactured products and waste as well as urban sprawl, overcrowding and pollution have wreaked environmental devastation. However, despite all the bad news, it is extraordinarily easy for us to reduce our carbon footprint. As designers and consumers, we can choose to combine the best of modern technology with traditional craftsmanship. We can apply existing knowledge and technology towards energy conservation, material efficiency, clean energy production, and sustainable working practises by choosing products that challenge the direction of contemporary design while also treading lightly on the planet.

KEY TO ICONS:

To help you to see at-a-glance the eco-credentials of the featured products, each is accompanied by one or more of the following icons:

## Biodegradable

Applies to products whose organic substances can be returned to the earth at the end of their life and broken down by other living organisms.

## Fairtrade

Refers to products that have been produced in an environment that guarantees decent, dignified working conditions, fair pay and sustainable development for the workers and craftspeople involved. Note that products carrying the fairtrade icon are not necessarily accredited by the Fairtrade Foundation, but do comply with criteria for fairly traded products.

## Locally Sourced

Using locally sourced materials reduces air miles, energy and packaging materials as well as helping support local industry. Many people are aware of the advantages of eating locally sourced food and the same benefits can be applied to using locally sourced materials.

## Low Energy ⚡

Products with the Low Energy icon are found mostly in the Lighting chapter. Low energy light bulbs use less than 20 percent of the energy of a conventional light bulb and last up to 15 times longer, while LED bulbs offer even greater savings, consuming less energy and offering up to 60,000 hours of use. Switching to low energy or LED bulbs is the easiest way for you to immediately lessen your carbon footprint.

## Low Waste ▦

Products with this icon use their waste materials responsibly. By reusing or recycling off-cuts, or by cleverly designing products so little waste is produced, designers reduce the amount of waste their manufacturing techniques create.

## No Toxins

Products made from organically grown materials or products containing no harmful chemicals carry the No Toxins icon.

## Recyclable

If a product is recyclable, it can be turned into a fresh supply of raw material at the end of its useful life. Many materials, including glass, paper, plastic, metal, textiles and electronics are recyclable. Although recycling is a positive move forward, it does require vast amounts of energy and it is not enough for us to simply rely on everything we use being recycled at the end of its life. Therefore the products that carry this icon also have additional eco benefits that further reduce their impact on the environment.

## Recycled

As we all continue to produce unacceptable amounts of waste, many designers are looking at ways in which they can process old materials into new products, in order to prevent the waste of potentially useful materials. In the strictest sense recycling produces a fresh supply of the same material, e.g. glass, paper, plastic, metal and textiles. Critics often claim that recycling also wastes vast amounts of energy, so many designers also salvage materials, reusing them directly in new products and thus conserving the energy it would take to recycle.

## Well Managed Resources

For us to live in an environmentally responsible way, the earth's resources must be used at a rate at which they can be replenished. The products carrying this icon are made from well managed resources including bamboo, Forest Stewardship Council (FSC) approved timber, and 100 percent pure wool. When buying products made from renewable materials, it is important to consider not just what they are made of, but how the material was harvested and how it was treated following its harvest.

# Furniture

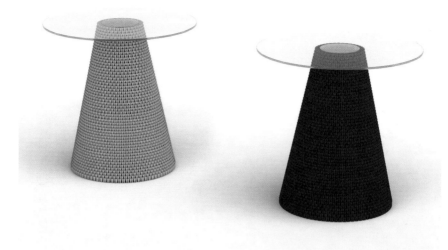

### Zipzi table, Michael Young, Established & Sons

Michael Young's Zipzi table for Established & Sons has a glass top supported on a conical base of recycled paper. www.establishedand sons.com

### Interlock Table, Interlock Furniture

Supporting a glass top on sustainable birch-veneered plywood, the slotted construction method of the Interlock Table allows it to be assembled without adhesives, fixtures or fittings. www.interlockfurniture.co.uk

### Three Short Planks coffee table, Sam Hoey, Benchmark

The glass top of Sam Hoey's coffee table gives a clear view of the clever interlocking supports, created in either sustainable oak or ash with a natural, non-toxic oiled finish. www.benchmark-furniture.com

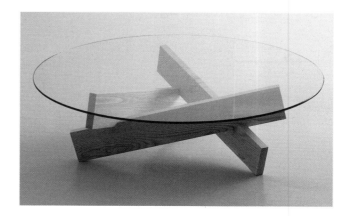

## Flytip table, Alexena Cayless

Dumped and abandoned furniture is rescued
from skips and given a new lease of life in
Alexena Cayless' 'Flytip' range. Cleaned up and
repainted, it is ready to be used all over again.
www.farmdesigns.co.uk

## Table, Claire Coles

Claire Coles uses
delicate embroidery to
transform disused and
unwanted furniture.
Her fragile motifs
make a surprising
contrast to the solidity
of the table.
www.clairecoles
design.co.uk

## Drunken table, Andrew Oliver

Andrew Oliver uses salvaged and secondhand
furniture to create his Drunken table. The surface
concertinas as if the wood has been folded like
paper or card. The legs appear weak in the
knees with traditional wood-turned forms cut and
rejoined to zigzag their way to the floor.
www.andrewoliverdesignsandmakes.co.uk

### Flip Table,
### Flip Furniture

Made from
sustainably sourced
timber, Flip Furniture's
space-saving and
versatile coffee table
transforms into
a dining table by
removing the base
and extending the
fold-down legs.
www.flipfurniture.com

### Brancusi table,
### Enrico Tonucci, Triangolo

The cracks, nails and gnarls of this table are a
reaction to the perfection and sterility of modern
furniture. The base is crafted from 200-year-old
solid oak roof beams and proudly displays all the
characteristics and history of a living material.
www.triangolo.com

### Elefant table,
### Sixixis

The Sixixis ethos is deeply rooted in sustainability,
the promotion and use of locally sourced timber
and sound environmental processes. The twisted
Elefant table is part of a small, limited-edition run
of steam-bent and screen-printed furniture.
www.sixixis.com

### Blox tables, Richard Whawell

The ultimate statement of simplicity, the Blox table relies on the natural beauty and character of sustainable solid oak for its timeless appeal.
www.oneecohome.co.uk

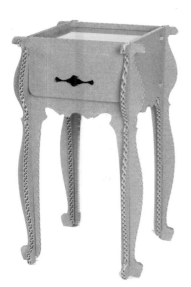

### Sidetable-C, Giles Miller, Dovetusai

Antique furniture design meets environmentally friendly thinking in this side table by Giles Miller, produced from recycled or sustainably sourced cardboard.
www.gilesmiller.com
www.dovetusai.com

### Living Object table/stool, Philip Henderson

Hand produced from 100 percent recycled paper and coated with a plant-based sealant, Living Object is a non-specific furniture item and can be used as a seat, table or stool.
www.philiphendersonstudio.co.uk

### Vitória table, Carlos Motta

Simple yet luxurious, the Vitória table is made in highly polished reclaimed solid lyptus. It is cleverly cut to show off the beauty and heavily banded grain of this reclaimed tropical hardwood.
www.carlosmotta.com.br

### Hoop table, Pli Design

An elegant occasional table with soft lines and simple curves, Hoop is made from laminated sustainable bamboo and finished with non-toxic hardwax oil.
www.plidesign.co.uk

### One Day Paper Waste table, Jens Praet, Droog

Droog concedes that the positive action of recycling a day's wasted paper from an office to make a table cast in toxic resin presents an ethical dilemma. It does, however, prompt discussion and argument on ecological issues.
www.droog.com

### Fold Table, Malcolm Baker

Made in sustainably sourced sycamore from a local estate, the timber in Malcolm Baker's Fold Table is sawn and dried where it is felled, keeping transit to a minimum.
www.malcolmbaker.co.uk

### I Was Here table, Jason Miller, Jason Miller Studio

Made from recycled plastic lumber, Jason Miller's I Was Here table is inscribed with graffiti culled from the tabletops and benches of New York City.
www.millerstudio.us

### Precious Famine table, Toni Grillo, Christofle

Toni Grillo recycles Parisian silversmith Christofle's cutlery in this ironic table.
www.christofle.com

### Till Death Do Us Part table, Martino d'Esposito and Franck Bragigand, Droog

As a protest against the disposable nature of furniture, it is hard to beat the lifetime contract binding owners of Droog's Till Death do us Part to their table. To ensure that the table has continuous appeal, it has been built with fold-out leaves to make it as versatile as possible. www.droog.com

### Pull Out Table, Anna McConnell

Rather than treating items as disposable, the Pull Out Table embodies Anna McConnell's belief in investing in and valuing good craftsmanship and adjusting it when necessary. This sustainable wood table expands to meet the needs of a growing family. www.annamcconnell.co.uk

### Bambu table, Henrik Tjaerby, Artek

Made entirely from bent bamboo veneer, the Bambu table exploits the characteristics of this under-used and sustainable plant material. www.artek.fi

### Duke table, Freshwest

Named in honour of Hawaiian surfing titan and Olympic swimmer Duke Kahanomoku, the Duke table by Freshwest draws inspiration from classic 1950s surfboard design. Combining local and sustainably sourced ash and cherry with driftwood, the table's laminated stripes evoke the golden age of surfing.
www.freshwest.co.uk

### Biblioteque table, Terence Conran, The Conran Shop

Made from sustainable oak, the Biblioteque collection is manufactured in workshops heated by burning timber off-cuts, which would otherwise go to waste. Long and sleek, the table seats up to ten people, and is built to last.
www.conran.com

### Nelson Round table, Terence Conran, Benchmark

Made from sustainable oak with a natural, non-toxic oiled finish, the Nelson Round is a plain yet elegant pedestal dining table which comfortably seats six.
www.benchmark-furniture.com

## Arris table,
## Gala Wright, MARK

The Arris dining table, made from solid
sustainable oak, features a unique three-way
bridle joint as a distinct feature.
www.markproduct.com

## Light Extending Table,
## Matthew Hilton

Matthew Hilton's Light Extending Table is
constructed using only sustainable timbers from
well managed forests.
www.matthewhilton.com

## Yum Yum table,
## Doha Chebib, Loyal Loot

Canadian collective Loyal Loot's Yum Yum table is
constructed from sustainably sourced cork. The
table also doubles as a storage unit, providing a
useful shelf for books and magazines.
www.loyalloot.com

## ECAL table,
## Nicolas Le Moigne

Manufactured from Eternit, a mixture of cement and recycled paper fibres, the ECAL table is made from a single wet sheet, creased for strength, and draped over a positive mould until dry. All the leftover pieces of Eternit are then made into flowerpots.
www.nicolaslemoigne.com

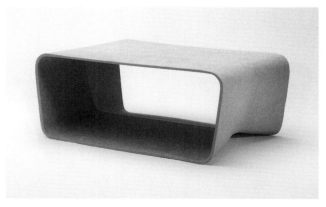

## Kite Table,
## Malcolm Baker

Inspired by the shape of a classic box kite, Malcolm Barker's table is made from two different types of recycled plastic sheet. The light material in the centre is made from yoghurt pots, while the darker material is made from black, gold and white coat hangers.
www.malcolmbaker.co.uk

## Kada stool/table,
## Yves Behar, Fuse Project

Made of recycled corrugated cardboard and transported flat-packed to save energy, this versatile piece of furniture can be used as a table, a stool or a storage unit.
www.fuseproject.com

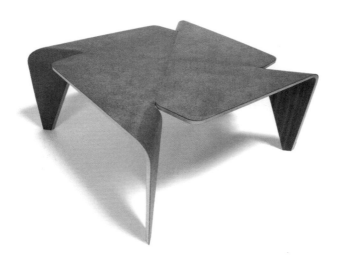

### Four Birds table, Simon Mount, Doistrinta

Inspired by airline logos and stylized drawings of birds from the 1950s, Simon Mount's Four Birds table is constructed from cork and birch ply with a walnut-veneered finish. The cork is treated with several layers of non-toxic varnish, giving the table an aged leather appearance.
www.designfactory.org

### Tatami table, Simon Mount, Doistrinta

This low coffee table is constructed from sustainable cork with a natural, non-toxic finish. The cork is strong, very hardwearing and waterproof.
www.designfactory.org

### Rekindle table, Inmodern

Constructed from just three pieces of FSC certified SmartWood and finished in non-toxic stains, the Rekindle coffee table ships flat-packed and slots together without the need for any tools or adhesives.
www.inmodern.net

## I-Beam Side Table, Matthew Hilton

Matthew Hilton's I-Beam Side Table is constructed from sustainably sourced solid American black walnut or American white oak.
www.matthewhilton.com

## Arbol table, Godoylab

The Arbol table is part of a collection from Godoylab using certified woods, which are laminated to promote biodegrading. Eight identical pieces are joined centrally to imitate the trunk and branches of trees, and finished with eco-friendly varnish.
www.godoylab.com

## Legend table, Christophe Delcourt, Roche Bobois

Made from naturally finished sustainable French oak, the Legend table is an example of Roche Bobois' commitment to ensuring minimal environmental impact. The table is designed using traditional cabinet-making techniques, avoiding the use of any glue, and is flat-packed for transportation and then assembled on-site by experts.
www.roche-bobois.com

### Alder Round table, Brent Comber

Ensuring minimal environmental impact, each Alder Round table is made from waste wood from forest clearances. Using the entire tree from trunk to twigs, the varying size of branches within each piece replicate the dappled light and shade of natural woodland. www.brentcomber.com

### Once a Ladder table, Claire Heather-Danthois

Making no attempt to hide its origins, the Once a Ladder table uses reclaimed timber in its rawest state for maximum simplicity and striking effect. Using the already-secured rungs for legs, and steel cable to hold the top together means no glue or complicated jointing is required. www.coroflot.com

### TOM desk, Sebastian Bergne, Triangolo

The TOM is a versatile desk made in sustainable oak and natural materials. The folding upper panel also allows it to double in width and transform into a useful table. www.triangolo.com

## Yellow Star table, Regis-R

Known as the 'Prince of Plastic', French designer Regis-R, collects waste plastic and recycles it into humorous products that question our rampant consumption.
r.egis.online.fr

## Drip Pattern Coffee Table, Caroline Till

With her ever present theme of renewal, the Drip Pattern Coffee Table is made from a salvaged table and is a perfect example of how Caroline Till seeks to reinvent otherwise discarded objects.
caroline@carolinetill.com

## Bailey table, Peter Lowe, Benchmark

Made from sustainably sourced timber, Peter Lowe's Bailey coffee table has an oak frame, which supports either an oak, stone or copper top.
www.benchmark-furniture.com

## Victoria table, Terence Conran, Benchmark

A robust dining table by Terence Conran in solid, sustainable oak, the Victoria seats eight comfortably and features a scrubbed top and oiled legs.
www.benchmark furniture.com

## Light Oval Table,
## Matthew Hilton

Constructed using sustainably sourced timbers,
Matthew Hilton's Light Oval Table is available
in engineered solid American black walnut or
engineered American white oak.
www.matthewhilton.com

## GB desk,
## Alexandra
## Sten
## Jørgensen

Inspired by the form
of an antique writing
desk, Alexandra
Sten Jørgensen's
sustainable design
addresses the way in
which furniture forms
are increasingly being
lost as technology
develops.
annealexandra@
gmail.com

## Waste Material table,
## Piet Hein Eek

As part of Piet Hein Eek's waste material project,
his table is made entirely from leftover steel
sheeting. Hundreds of scraps are laboriously
bent into box shapes and assembled like a
jigsaw, achieving a truly unique result.
www.pietheineek.nl

## Lack table, Ikea

Despite its solid appearance, the Lack table features a hollow board-on-frame construction with recycled paper inside. Not only does this method save materials, but it is also very light, therefore saving energy in transportation.
www.ikea.com

## Heerema table, Plexwood

Plexwood is constructed by gluing vertical layers of wood together to create a material with a distinctive linear structure. With a top of solid Plexwood, the Heerema table is the perfect demonstration of this sustainable, locally sourced and toxin-free material.
www.plexwood.nl

## Norbert o table, Woodloops

Constructed from local FSC-certified cherry or oak, the Norbert o table is designed to be as solid as possible while using the absolute minimum amount of timber.
www.woodloops.de

### Map Table,
### Bombus, All Things Original

Bombus revive the Victorian tradition of découpage on reused coffee tables. Covered in old maps, comics and posters, each piece is unique.
www.allthingsoriginal.com

### Flute table,
### Giles Miller

By splicing sustainably sourced or recycled cardboard, Giles Miller creates the fluted effect which gives his table its name. Fluting creates organic patterns, which have the effect of softening the table's bold shape.
www.gilesmiller.com

### Flat Pack Table,
### Freshwest

Freshwest were as environmentally aware as possible when designing their Flat Pack Table. All wood is sourced locally from wind-fallen trees and no glue or screws are used, only wooden pegs or wedges. The table is also finished in a natural non-toxic finish and, of course, comes flat-packed.
www.freshwest.co.uk

## Generoso Parmegiani table, Generoso Design

Arriving flat-packed and made entirely of double-strength recycled cardboard, Generoso Design's table is available in a range of sizes and is able to support over 80kg (176lb) in weight.
www.generosodesign.it

## Don't Spill your Coffee table, David Graas

Working on the understanding that all products are temporary, David Graas ensures that his designs are as harmless as possible when they inevitably come to be discarded. Not only is Don't Spill your Coffee recyclable, it comes flat-packed and can simply be slotted together.
www.davidgraas.com

## Table, Karen Ryan

Karen Ryan spends her time rummaging through skips to find discarded and unwanted furniture that she can transform into products such as this banded table.
www.bykarenryan.co.uk

## Barrel table, Estudio Gandia

The Barrel table achieves a highly machined look with minimal effort by using a reused stainless steel washing machine drum as a base. The drum also acts as a diffuser for the internal light.
www.estudiogandia.com.ar

## Love table, Stephen Burks, Cappellini

Making the most of the office shredder, the 'Love' collection of service tables is handmade in recycled paper and comes in a range of sizes.
www.cappellini.it

## Either Oar table/raft, David Cameron and Toby Hadden, & Made

Emphasizing the issue of climate change, this sustainable dining table quickly transforms into a buoyant raft, with the detachable legs becoming oars, in the event of a flash flood.
www.and-made.com

### Reveal table, Ku Designs

The Reveal is a distinctive coffee table, moulded in sustainable birch plywood. The internal shelf is created by separating the laminated timber, revealing one of a range of vibrant colours, all of which contrast with the natural wood veneer.
www.ku-designs.com

### Parati table, Carlos Motta

Available as either a dining table or a table-bench, the Parati is constructed from reclaimed peroba rosa. The natural, simple style of the table recalls the Brazilian beaches that provide much of the inspiration for Carlos Motta's designs.
www.carlosmotta.com.br

### Keystone table, Partridge & Walmsley, Benchmark

Partridge & Walmsley's Keystone coffee table is stylish yet sturdy, and constructed from sustainably sourced solid oak.
www.benchmark-furniture.com

### Upper Kaibito table, Ryan Frank

An attempt to use salvaged materials in mass production, Ryan Frank's dining table from his 'Strata' collection is constructed from a mix of chipboard from discarded and battered office furniture and FSC-certified birch ply.
www.ryanfrank.net

### A Ply table, Peter Masters, Burnt Toast

Burnt Toast's A Ply table is typical of Peter Masters' ability to create deceptively simple yet sophisticated design using single sheets of sustainable plywood. Manufacturing is executed with a minimum of powered machinery and finished in environmentally friendly water-based paints.
www.burnttoastdesign.co.uk

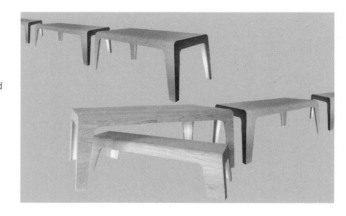

### YBA table, Peter Masters, Burnt Toast

Designed with clever use of sustainable plywood, the YBA coffee table has Y-shaped legs and is available in a range of sizes and veneers.
www.burnttoastdesign.co.uk

## Dugout Canoe Table, Rob van Acker

Working with local craftspeople, Rob van Acker creates tables from dilapidated dugout canoes mounted on welded frames. Made in Zambia from local hardwoods, the canoes eventually become too cracked to float and would have otherwise been used as firewood.
www.robvanacker.com

## Atlas table, Hannes Gumpp

Just as Atlas carried the heavens on his shoulders, Hannes Gumpp's table of the same name employs reused cardboard tubes to support a slab of Greek marble. Despite having been used, the tubes are in perfect condition because they were protected by rolls of carpet in their previous incarnation.
www.hannesgumpp.com

## AIUE stool/ side table, Em2

While the base of the AIUE stool is made from certified jequitiba wood, the seat is created from recycled magazine pages by community artists in Brazil, ensuring that each item is unique.
www.em2design.com

### Recycled mobile phone table, Noel Hennessy

A unique plastic formed from recycled mobile phone cases distinguishes the top of Noel Hennessy's table. Each piece is unique and features a frame made from sustainable Scottish oak.
www.noelhennessy.com

### Potentially Lasting Table, Philip Henderson

Using a minimal amount of locally felled hardwood as a framework, Philip Henderson's Potentially Lasting Table features a top made of pasta, demonstrating the tasty potential of this low-energy material.
www.philiphenderson studio.co.uk

### Leaf Tables, Russel Pinch, Benchmark

Available in a range of sizes and sustainable woods including oak, cherry and walnut, Benchmark's trio of occasional Leaf Tables evokes the magic of the forest floor.
www.benchmark furniture.com

### Banco de Amedoim table, Carlos Motta

By reusing discarded timber in his Amedoim table, Carlos Motta is able to work in beautiful hardwoods without contributing to the destruction of threatened habitats.
www.carlosmotta.com.br

### Camburi sideboard, Carlos Motta

Made from peroba rosa, a timber from his native Brazil, Carlos Motta's Camburi sideboard makes use of a glass top to show off the striking colour of this beautiful reclaimed hardwood.
www.carlosmotta.com.br

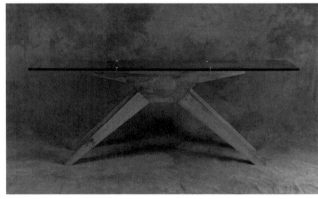

### Coffee table, Andy Wood

Made with sturdy blocks of reclaimed timber, Andy Wood's coffee tables are available in either elm or oak salvaged from Chatham docks.
www.andywood.eu

## Reclaimed oak and slate table, One Eco Home

Made from locally sourced reclaimed materials, this dining table celebrates the flaws of its natural materials. Beautifully cracked and knotted, the Devonshire oak is finished in vegetable-based oil and assembled with environmentally friendly glue. The slate is treated with non-toxic sealant.
www.oneecohome.co.uk

## Split It table, Peter Masters, Burnt Toast

Combining beautiful walnut veneer with sustainable birch ply, this versatile table can be rearranged to suit individual needs.
www.burnttoastdesign.co.uk

## Coffee table, Nick Rawcliffe, Raw Studio

Made from recycled coffee grounds and cast with resin, Raw Studio's Coffee table is available with an embossed, flat or satin surface, supported on steel legs.
www.rawstudio.co.uk

## Final Stand table,
## Peter Masters, Burnt Toast

With its clear glass top, the Final Stand table creates the illusion of having four gently inclined, unsupported legs. The table comes in a number of sizes and with a choice of different legs, all of which are either recycled or made from FSC-managed timber and finished in vinegar stain or non-toxic tung oil.
www.burnttoastdesign.co.uk

## Truss Table,
## Jonathan Tibbs

This branch-like Truss Table is available in sycamore, ash or oak with walnut detailing, all sustainably sourced from local sawmills.
www.johnathantibbs.com

## Traffic table,
## Ryan Frank

Left for an hour on a public pathway and then mounted on a base of FSC-certified plywood, the recyclable polypropolene top of Ryan Frank's mobile coffee table represents a grubby snapshot of commuting in London.
www.ryanfrank.net

## Thin Side Table, Matthew Hilton

Matthew Hilton's Thin Side Table is constructed from sustainably sourced solid American black walnut or American white oak.
www.matthewhilton.com

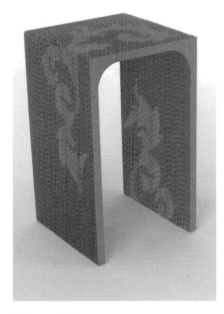

## Flute table, Giles Miller

Made from either sustainably sourced or recycled cardboard, Giles Miller's Flute side table has an elegance not normally associated with cardboard furniture.
www.gilesmiller.com

## Table, Scrap Design

Scrap Design reuse locally sourced materials to highlight the throwaway culture of modern times. With a glass top bolted onto an unwanted washing machine drum, this table makes no attempt to hide its origins.
www.scrapdesign.co.uk

## Tree Fork Table,
## Rob van Acker

After personally constructing the base and framework, Rob van Acker's Tree Fork Tables are taken to a nearby village in Western Province, Zambia and completed using the expertise of local weavers.
www.robvanacker.com

## Dining Table,
## Oliver Tilbury

Constructed using FSC certified ash and naturally ebonized English oak, Oliver Tilbury's Dining Table is all about balance, with the legs and top supporting and bracing one another. This is made possible by a cunning joint system within the apex of the legs which also allows the table to be completely flat-packed.
www.olivertilbury.com

## Anticipation
## No Explosives
## folding table,
## Wyssem and
## Cecile Nochi

The darkly humorous Anticipation No Explosives by Lebanese designers Wyssem and Cecile Nochi, lies somewhere between design and art. The folding side table is topped with a poignant reused road sign warning of possible bomb blasts.
www.wyssemnochi.com

## Cover Stool,
## Branex Design, Montis

For maximum material efficiency, the packaging of the Cover Stool is a cardboard box which then transforms into the product itself. The stool is then covered in a unique sustainable textile, specially developed by Kvadrat.
www.montis.nl

## Streep bench,
## A4A Design

Made from recycled honeycombed corrugated cardboard, and laminated bench tops, the Streep bench is a sturdy, fun and eco-efficient solution to seating.
www.a4adesign.it

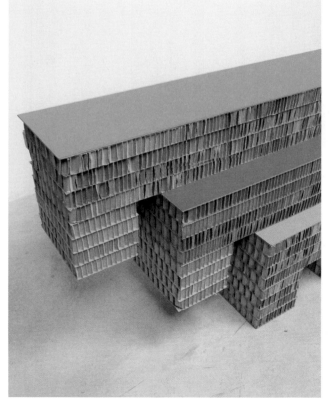

## Wood stool,
## Pol's Potten

Handcrafted by the Laobe tribe, who live on the outskirts of Senegal, Pol's Potten's Wood stools are made of sustainably harvested cordyla pinnata wood, which can only be taken from trees that have died from drought or old age. The wood is sculpted using traditional tools, and either left untreated or polished with beeswax.
www.polspotten.nl

## Re-form Chair,
## Aaron Moore,
## Re-form Furniture

The Re-Form Chair comprises a beech frame with
a seat of recycled, high-density polyethylene.
Grown locally, the beech is seasoned in a solar
kiln, while the polyethylene is made from waste
shampoo and detergent bottles.
www.re-formfurniture.com

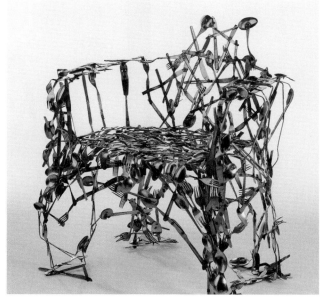

## Cutlery Chair,
## Osian Batyka

Some restaurants change their cutlery as often
as every nine months. The Cutlery Chair utilizes
these hard-to-recycle, unwanted cutlery pieces
as building blocks to create unique pieces of
furniture that are works of art..
www.osianbatykawilliams.com

## Tandem Acolyte seating,
## Eco Systems

Comprising 14 standard components, Tandem
can be configured to produce any number
of contract chairs, benches or tables. Made
of sustainable bamboo, 100 percent natural
biodegradable latex  wool and recyclable
aluminium hardware, the system is also flat-
packed for easy transportation.
www.ecosystemsbrand.com

### Olivia chair, Max McMurdo, Reestore

Reestore have modified the backrest of the Olivia, previously a plain folding wooden chair, allowing it to double as a clothes hanger.
www.reestore.com

### Bambu stackable chair, Henrik Tjærby, Artek

An extraordinary plant, bamboo has twice the compressive strength of concrete and the same tensile strength-to-weight ratio as steel. This versatile, renewable and incredibly strong material is an underused resource in contemporary design. Artek's stackable bent-bamboo veneer chair illustrates how sustainable furniture can also be technically innovative.
www.artek.fi

### Alder Saddle stool, Brent Comber

One of the first species to appear after deforestation, alder enriches the soil and encourages the rebirth of the forest. Rather than harvesting alder from areas of regrowth, Brent Comber seeks out strands from deforested areas. He then uses the entire tree – from trunk to branches, right down to the twigs. When all that is left is woodchips and sawdust, Comber returns it to the soil via a composting facility.
www.brentcomber.com

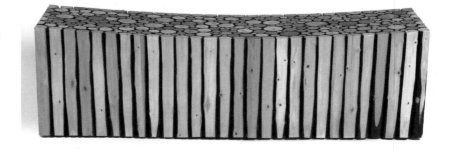

## RD Legs chair, Cohda

Hand woven from 100 percent recycled domestic plastic waste, the RD Legs chair is considered an iconic piece of eco design. A result of Cohda's experiments with recycled plastic processes, the chair is available in a limited edition of 50 numbered and signed pieces. www.cohda.com

## Subway chair, Boris Bally

Bringing a new meaning to getting a seat on the subway, Borris Bally's aluminium Subway chairs are made using hand-fabricated, pierced and brake-formed recycled New York subway signs. www.borisbally.com

## Inkuku chair, Ryan Frank

Named after the Zulu word for chicken, Ryan Frank's Inkuku chair is based on the traditional African approach of using everyday discarded plastics to make objects for the home. Through this design Frank aims to create awareness about the excess use of plastic grocery bags. www.ryanfrank.net

## Inter-B-Lock chair, Julienne Dolphin-Wilding

Julienne Dolphin-Wilding breathes new life into refuse that would otherwise be burned or consigned to landfill, fashioning English yew into Lego-like bricks to create the Inter-B-Lock chair. The self-assembly kit can be used to create an armchair, bench, table, stool or pedestals.
www.dolphinwilding.com

## This Side Up occasional stool, David Graas

Designer David Graas believes that 'good design' is embodied by a product that functions just as well as garbage at the end of its life as it does while in use, and will not cause problems for the environment. By choosing cardboard as the sole material for This Way Up, it can be easily dismantled and composted at the end of its life.
www.davidgraas.com

## SIE25 chair, Pawel Grunert

A marriage of organic and industrial materials is demonstrated by the SIE25 chair, which successfully juxtaposes stainless steel and straw to form a striking and sculptural seat.
www.grunert.art.pl

## Tetris dining chair, WEmake

Rather than making the Tetris dining chair and then transporting it themselves, WEmake provide you with instructions on how to build your own chair from waste cardboard. Based around a 10cm (4in) grid, and demonstrating what is possible with even the simplest of shapes, the profile is designed to save resources and get you involved in making your own furniture.
www.wemake.co.uk

### Vinco chair, Toni Grillo, Susdesign

The Vinco chair is made from cork, a natural and ecological material. Using CNC milling technology, the product represents an eco-efficient solution to contemporary seating. www.susdesign.com

### Palette chair, Nina Tolstrup

Rather than making and shipping the Palette chair, Nina Tolstrup sells the instructions on how to create her chair yourself, relying on the idea that pallets are a generic product found everywhere in the world. This allows the consumer to source their own waste materials and build their own chair locally. www.studiomama.com

### Sting chair, Fredrik Mattson and Stefan Borselius, Blå Station

Created without screws, glue or rivets, the Sting chair is created from 70 percent reclaimed aluminium. The concept behind the design is one of simplicity, resulting in two aluminium profiles – one for the backrest and one for the seat – linked together by a simple snap-lock fitting. www.blastation.se

## Elefant Stool, Sixixis

The Sixixis ethos is deeply rooted in sustainability, the promotion and use of locally sourced timber and sound environmental processes. The twisted Elefant Stool is part of a small, limited-edition run, of steam-bent and screen-printed stools.
www.sixixis.com

## Custom Made chair, Karen Ryan

Using discarded chairs found in skips or junk shops as her raw material, Karen Ryan transforms unwanted furniture into something more desirable.
www.bykarenryan.co.uk

## Map Chair, Bombus, All Things Original

Using traditional découpage techniques, Bombus completely re-cover old and unwanted furniture in maps, comics or old posters. Every product is unique as each chair features a different selection of images and text.
www.allthingsoriginal.com

## Rag chair, Tejo Remy, Droog

Made from the contents of 15 bags of rags, each Tejo Remy Rag chair is unique. The chair arrives readymade but the user has the option to recycle their own discarded clothes into the design.
www.droog.com

## Art Deco Armchair, Squint

Squint reupholster disused and unwanted furniture with a colourful patchwork of vintage fabrics. Each design is unique, yet united by the signature Squint aesthetic. This Art Deco armchair has been reupholstered with vintage ticking and English silks.
www.squintlimited.com

## Made In Chair, Pieces of You

Pieces of You comment on the wasteful and unethical nature of sourcing trade and materials abroad by means of the textile design on their Made In Chair. Printed on organic hemp-cotton canvas, the textile is used to upholster a reconditioned 1970s chair.
www.piecesofyou.co.uk

## Alt Chair,
## Aaron Moore,
## Re-form Furniture

Made of locally grown ash that is bent while it is still green for maximum energy efficiency, the Alt Chair also has a seat of recycled, high-impact polystyrene made of waste coffee cups and the material found inside fridges.
www.re-formfurniture.co.uk

## Vanity easy chair,
## Lisa Widén and Anna
## Innarchos, WIS Designs

WIS Designs make unique pieces out of used and neglected parts from old products. This easy chair is reupholstered in pieces of old leather cut from out-of-style jackets and coats. The natural, aged patina of the leather gives the chair an instant 'lived in' feel.
www.wisdesign.se

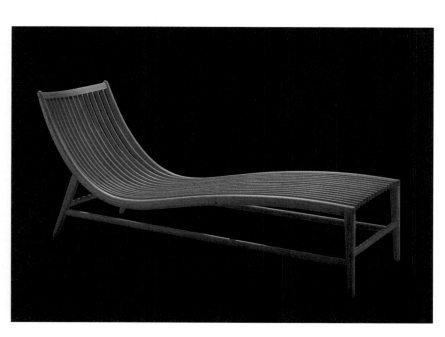

## Agatha Dreams chaise longue,
## Christophe Pillet, Ceccotti

Constructed using sustainable hardwoods and natural non-toxic lacquers and glues, Christophe Pillet's chaise longue is an elegant and sustainable design.
www.ceccotticollezioni.it

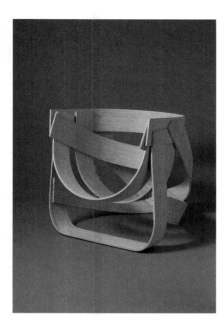

## Bamboo Chair, Remy Veenhuizen

Constructed from steam-bent, fast-growing bamboo, Remy Veenhuizen's sculptural chair is both sustainable and recyclable.
www.remyveenhuizen.nl

## Dondo rocking chaise longue, Generoso Design

Dondo is made from double-corrugated cardboard. Thanks to the particular shape of the rocking chair, you can change your position from sitting to lying down by moving your arms forwards or backwards.
www.generoso design.it

## Knit Chair, Emiliano Godoy, Godoylab, Pirwi

Containing only natural and biodegradable components, the Knit Chair comprises FSC certified birch and maple plywood, finished in natural Livos varnish, and strong yet flexible cotton rope connections, allowing it to adapt to the user's body shape and movements.
www.pirwi.com

## Wanda chaise longue, A4A Design

The Wanda chaise longue is constructed from recycled honeycombed corrugated cardboard, and wool felt. The result is a strong, sustainable and comfortable chair.
www.a4adesign.it

## Cabbage Chair, Nendo

Designed for an exhibition curated by Issey Miyake in Tokyo, the Cabbage Chair is created from scraps of the mass-produced pleated paper he is famed for. Unfinished, assembled without nails or screws and with no internal structure, the chair appears naturally as its outside layers are peeled away. Its strength is derived from resins added during the original paper production process.
www.nendo.jp

## Bug Chair, Lou Rota

The classic Robin Day chair has been given the Fairy Godmother treatment by Lou Rota, and transformed into a new design crawling with bugs. The result is a gritty, witty and pretty modern-day fairytale.
www.lourota.com

## Timur, Katia Stewart

Timur is a large curvaceous chair made with steam-bent sustainably sourced rattan. The chair moves easily between indoors or outdoors, blurring the definition of traditional garden furniture.
www.katiastewart.com

## Annie chair, Max McMurdo, Reestore

The sight of shopping trolleys dumped in otherwise beautiful rivers and canals inspired Max McMurdo to transform them into furniture. He now focuses on using damaged or dented trolleys, which are often thrown away by supermarkets when the wheels stop working.
www.reestore.com

## Gordon chair, Max McMurdo, Reestore

The Gordon chair is inspired by the British, tea-drinking builder. Not only does it utilize otherwise useless reject wheelbarrow pans, but it also sits firmly on a chrome base salvaged from old office chairs.
www.reestore.com

## White Plastic Chair, Tina Roeder

The White Plastic Chair forms part of a series of disused and decaying garden chairs which Tina Roeder has elevated from the ordinary by individually perforating and sanding each one. The result is a highly collectible and beautiful chair.
www.tineroeder.com

## Tape chair, El Ultimo Grito

Sourcing all materials from waste, limited edition Tape chairs are made out of discarded mattresses and cardboard boxes bound and upholstered with multi-coloured electrical tape.
www.elultimogrito.co.uk

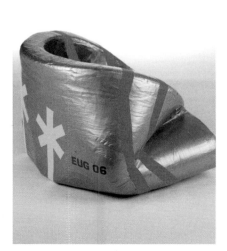

## Lightweight chair,
## Oliver van der Breggen

Produced using FSC certified timbers, Oliver van der Breggen's chair is designed to be as lightweight as possible. Beautifully handcrafted using minimal materials, the seat and backrest are light but robust due to their method of construction. The strong double tenon joints within the maple frame also add to the chair's elegant design. All glues used are non-toxic and environmentally friendly.
ollyvdb@hotmail.com

## Evora lounger,
## Simon Mount, Doistrinta

A much under-used resource, cork can be applied in innovative and unexpected ways to create warm, comfortable and sustainable contemporary furniture, such as the Evora lounger by Doistrinta.
www.designfactory.org.uk

## One Cut Chair,
## Scott Jarvie

The One Cut Chair is formed from a single sheet of sustainable plywood, using a high-pressure water-jet cutting technique. A single continuous incision produces a shape that is then folded into the seat and backrest. The design aims to make the most economical use of material possible, while minimizing the energy required for manufacture.
www.scottjarvie.co.uk

### Mr Clumsy chair, Simon Mount, Doistrinta

Mr Clumsy's unique qualities lie in its classic looks, fused with an innovative use of materials – combining cartoon-like spider legs with an oversized body of birch ply, cork and Zotefoam.
www.designfactory.org.uk

### DC chair, Interlock Furniture

By using sustainable walnut-veneered birch plywood and a unique slotted construction that allows the chair to be made without any fixtures or fittings, Interlock Furniture have created an easily assembled and ecologically sensitive chair.
www.interlockfurniture.co.uk

### Corks stools, Jasper Morrison, Moooi

A simple and elegant stool turned from agglomerate Portuguese cork, Morrison's design can be used as a small side table, a stool or an ottoman. Harvested by hand in an undamaging nine-year cycle, cork is a truly sustainable, recyclable and impermeable material.
www.moooi.com

## Rocking Chair, Sixixis

The Rocking Chair, made of steam-bent ash, forms part of a limited edition of 15 chairs, individually signed and numbered by the maker. The steam bending process employed by Sixixis offers a non-toxic, low-energy method of manipulating local, unseasoned timber. The vegetable-tanned leather seat is handcrafted by a local Cornish upholsterer. www.sixixis.com

## Hamaca chair, EM2

Constructed from certified tauari wood and vegetable-tanned leather, the Hamaca chair combines contemporary Brazilian design with traditional craftsmanship. Community artists work the leather using macramé knotting techniques to create a seat that will adjust over time to embrace the individual shape of the user. www.em2design.com

## Signature rocking chair, David Haig

Using sustainably sourced American black walnut grown in his native New Zealand, designer David Haig delicately steam-bends his timber in order to create the elegant curves of this rocking chair. www.centre-for-fine-woodworking.co.nz

## Primavera chair, Franca Heig, Vittorio Bonacina

Sustainable rattan is woven by hand to create Vittorio Bonacina's classic chair. Rattan is a fast-growing natural material that is ideal for furniture design, being strong, flexible and light.
www.bonacina vittorio.it

## Flexa chair, Carlos Motta

Brazilian designer Carlos Motta began creating furniture from driftwood washed ashore in São Paolo. He is now renowned for his environmentally sustainable designs, which are all created from recycled or reused wood. The Flexa chair is made from natural, vegetable-tanned leather and reused lyptus prime, a tropical hardwood.
www.carlosmotta.com.br

## Plaisance lounge chair and ottoman, Liana Cane, North South Project

North South Project works closely with manufacturers and craft producers in developing companies to create new design collections, highlighting the distinctive skills of each producer. Made in Guyana, the Plaisance chair and ottoman aims to promote rainforest conservation through the use of renewable forest products.
www.northsouthproject.com

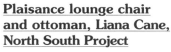

## Splash stool, Nick Barberton

Nick Barberton prides himself on making simple, modern furniture, crafted traditionally by hand. The Splash stool is constructed from sustainable and local sycamore or oak, using offcuts or waste left over from the designer's wood-burning stove at home.
www.nickbarberton.co.uk

## Viento stacking chair, Dondoli and Pocci, Bonaldo

Viento is a stacking chair made entirely of recyclable, air-moulded polypropylene. No paints or glues are used during the production process, and the air moulding technology reduces material usage by creating a chair of considerable strength and thickness, with a hollow inner core.
www.bonaldo.it

## The Family chair, Derek Welsh

Available in small, medium and large sizes, this solid, box-shaped chair is created from sustainably sourced Douglas fir. The provenance of Derek Welsh's timber is always an important consideration in his design process and he actively engages with environmentally sound replanting and harvesting practices.
www.derekwelsh.co.uk

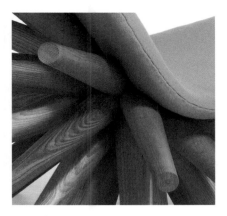

### Burst chair, Oliver Tilbury

The 31 legs of this chair in solid FSC certified ash don't just appear to merge together as if naturally formed – they really do merge together and intersect. The chair originated from discussions about function and necessity, simplicity and reason; what is honest and legitimate, impossible and possible, natural and illusionary.
www.olivertilbury.com

### Pinch Stool, Naughtone

The Pinch Stool has a solid hardwood frame of untreated sycamore or beech, sourced from a locally managed, renewable forest and padded with scraps of recycled foam. Coloured with natural dyes, the upholstery fabric is 100 percent wool from Bute Fabric, based on Scotland's Isle of Bute.
www.naughtone.com

### Pano chair, Studio Lo

Constructed by water-jet cutting a single piece of wood, the Pano chair uses a minimum of materials and is transported flat-packed to save energy. The chair's assembly, without any adhesive, is achieved with simple mortise and tenon joints.
studio.lo.neuf.fr

## 44 armchair, Natanel Gluska

Swiss furniture-maker Natanel Gluska uses sustainable wood and natural non-toxic finishes to create playful and rough-hewn pieces of furniture, such as this chunky, blocky armchair.
www.natanelgluska.com

## Log Stool, Shin and Tomoko Azumi, La Palma

Constructed from sustainable oak-veneered plywood with an aluminium frame, the Log Stool is both simple and sustainable.
www.lapalma.it

## Strata bench and stool, Werner Aisslinger, Purple South

Available in sustainable MDF or plywood, the Strata bench and stool is constructed with material efficiency in mind. The product is designed to assemble easily without any nails, screws or plastic fastenings, and is finished with water-based non-toxic paints.
www.purplesouth.com

### Dining chair,
### Matthew Hilton

This dining chair by Matthew Hilton is constructed using sustainably sourced oak and is finished with natural, non-toxic oils.
www.matthewhilton.com

### 3 Blocks nesting stools,
### Michaele Simmering
### and Johannes Pauwen,
### Kalon Studios

The versatility of form found in these nesting stools allows the user to find uses for every situation. Made of bamboo with a unique, non-toxic finish specially developed by Kalon Studios, the stools are manufactured to maximize time, labour and material efficiency. The nests can also be stacked for efficient transport and storage.
www.kalonstudios.com

### Isometric Chair,
### Michaele Simmering
### and Johannes Pauwen,
### Kalon Studios

The Isometric Chair melds the characteristics of bamboo with the precision of CNC milling. Made without hardware, the structural integrity of the chair relies upon the natural properties of bamboo and is made with 100 percent non-toxic and sustainable materials.
www.kalonstudios.com

## No Logo Piano Stool, Pieces of You

Pieces of You highlight the massive wastefulness of senseless consumption, using logo labels from cast-off clothing to reupholster an unused piano stool.
www.piecesofyou.
co.uk

## Baley bench, Gusto Design

Having long been used in building and furniture making, straw is an appealing and sustainable bulk material. Its use as a seat occurs naturally in the countryside and Baley formalizes this reappropriation, transforming the bale into a piece of domestic and hardwearing furniture with a made-to-measure transparent cover.
www.gustodesign.co.uk

## Urchin knitted ottoman, Flocks

These undyed, handknitted ottomans come with their own identity card so that the owner can trace the path of their soft seat's origins. Each unique identity card illustrates the breed of sheep, its provenance and the quantity of wool used. This simple and honest technique lets customers know, in a friendly way, where the materials have been sourced.
www.theseflocks.com

## Tapestry ottoman, Frederique Morrel

Based on the reworking of vintage needlework scavenged from secondhand shops, Frederique Morrel's ottoman gives subversive new meaning to tapestries that once took hours to make.
www.frederique morrel.com

## Oak Stool, David Sutton

Traditional mortise- and tenon-jointed, sustainable, PEFC certified European oak forms the sole component of David Sutton's steam-bent stool. Sourced in a green state, the timber can be supplied to its desired working size, reducing waste in the workshop.
www.davidsutton.co.uk

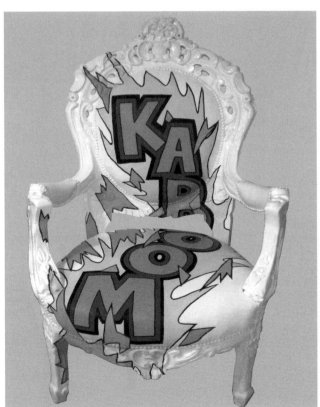

## Kaboom chair, Jimmie Martin

With their bold and impulsive graffiti-style artwork, Jimmie Martin restyle furniture bought from auctions and antique markets.
www.jimmiemartin. co.uk

## Simple bench and chair, Patty Johnson, Mabeo

Mabeo is committed to the production of high-end contemporary furniture in Botswana, Africa. The company's Simple bench and chair, designed by Patty Johnson as part of her North South Project, which helps Southern-hemisphere manufacturers find Northern-hemisphere markets for their products.
www.mabeofurniture.com

## ST04 stool, Backenzahntm, Philip Mainzer, e15

Made from four clearly recognizable, identical pieces of solid, sustainably sourced timber, this stool reveals the beauty of naturally finished wood. A slightly concave seat provides sitting comfort.
www.e15.com

## Treasure dining chair, Maarten Baas

Built using waste from a furniture factory, Maarten Baas' dining chair follows the form of its original source material. As the factory continues to produce their furniture they also reproduce identically-shaped waste, allowing Baas to continue creating his Treasure chairs.
www.maartenbaas.com

## Maun Windsor chair, Patty Johnson, Mabeo

This chair is handcrafted from wood harvested from well-managed forests and finished with a natural soap-flake finish. It melds classic shaker-inspired lines with the abstract quality of African sculpture and is manufactured as part of the North South Project, a fair trade project based in Botswana which brings long-term benefits to local craftspeople and their community.
www.mabeofurniture.com

## Jones stool, Woodloops

Handcrafted from FSC certified larch, Woodloops'
simple and honest Jones stool is also finished with
natural non-toxic oils.
www.woodloops.de

## Nobody chair, Komplot, HAY

Inspired by a cloth laid
over a chair to protect
it, the ghost-like
Nobody is produced
without a frame by
thermo-pressing 100
percent recyclable PET
felt mat, a material
produced from used
water bottles, in
a single process.
The production
requires no chemical
additives and no
additional materials
or reinforcement.
www.hay.dk

## Enorme Fauteuil armchair, Piet Hein Eek

Piet Hein Eek saves
timber from unwanted
and disused furniture
then reuses it to
construct the pieces
in his 'Scrap Wood'
series of furniture.
The original patina of
every piece of wood
is left untouched,
creating a wonderful
patchwork of effects
and finishes.
www.pietheineek.nl

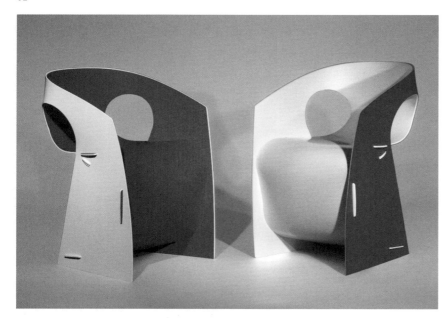

### i b pop chair,
### Blue Marmalade

Optimizing the properties of a single sheet of recyclable polypropylene, the free-flowing form and construction of i b pop eliminate the need for glue because the fixings are formed from the same sheet. This simple construction allows for easy recycling.
www.bluemarmalade.co.uk

### Raita bench,
### Eeva Lithovius, Durat

Durat is a solid polyester-based material used for custom made surfaces in public and private interiors. It contains recycled plastics and is itself 100 percent recyclable. The Raita bench highlights the variety of different colours in which Durat is available.
www.durat.com

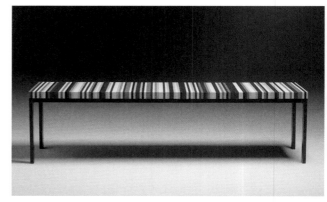

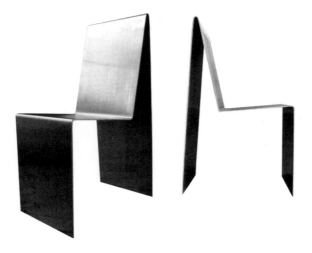

### Kina chair,
### Osvaldo Matos

Created as part of a 'Re-made in Portugal' exhibition, the chair is produced from 100 percent aluminium and comes packaged in 100 percent recycled cardboard packaging. This means that the chair is fully recyclable at the end of its life.
www.osvaldomatos.pt

## Aluminium Dining Chair, Rob van Acker

This aluminium dining chair is constructed from metal recycled from the many Land Rovers used in the village of Mongu, Zambia. When the Land Rovers finally die, local craftspeople turn them into pots and pans, but Rob van Acker uses the weather-beaten aluminum panels to make furniture.
www.robvanacker.com

## Jakkara stool, Eeva Lithovius, Durat

The Jakkara stool is made from Durat, a solid polyester-based material used for custom made surfaces in public and private interiors. It contains recycled plastics and is itself 100 percent recyclable.
www.durat.com

## 20-06 chair, Norman Foster, Emeco

The content of recycled aluminium used to make the 20-06 chair is 80 percent. Of the recycled aluminium, half is post-consumer (soft drink cans) and half is post-industrial (manufacturing scrap). Perhaps of even greater significance is the projected lifespan of the chair, estimated to last for 150 years or more.
www.emeco.net

## Thuthu stool,
## Patty Johnson, Mabeo

Made in Botswana under fairtrade conditions,
Mabeo's Thuthu stool merges African influences
with Patty Johnson's contemporary design
sensibilities.
www.mabeofurniture.com

## Bunson chair,
## Lino Codato Collection

The Bunson chair is completely woven from
water hyacinth, a natural fibre that grows in
abundance in Thailand. The water hyacinth
is harvested sustainably and responsibly in a
fairtrade environment.
www.icc-collection.com

## Cielo chair,
## Mikiya Kobayashi

This simple and beautiful chair offers a
contemporary alternative to traditional rattan.
The Cielo chair has a small frame that uses a
minimum of materials.
www.mikiyakobayashi.com

### Miss Gana Puff ottoman, Karin Wittmann Wilsmann, Brasil Faz Design

The Miss Gana Puff forms part of a fairtrade initiative providing employment in southern Brazil. The colourful strands that form the central component of this design are recycled from EVA rubber scraps discarded by Brazilian shoemaking industries.
www.brasilfazdesign.com.br

### Caught Pouffe, Barley Massey

Inspired by traditional fishermen's techniques, the Caught Pouffe is made by stretching knotted recycled bicycle inner tubes over a fabric beanbag. All the materials are locally sourced from business waste in east London.
www.fabrications1.co.uk

### Floral Chair, Lou Rota

Lou Rota takes vintage or salvaged furniture and transforms it with eclectic collage. The polypropylene Floral Chair has been covered in a colourful mix of flower photographs cut from seed catalogues and magazines and then sealed with an environmentally friendly, water-based varnish.
www.lourota.com

### Bamboo Chair,
### Lara de Greef

Fast-growing renewable bamboo is used to create Lara de Greef's simple and solid chair. Not only is it sustainable, but the material also offers an array of possibilities for advanced applications extending far beyond traditional bamboo handicraft products.
www.laradegreef.nl

### Bloc stool,
### Woodloops

Bloc clearly illustrates Woodloops' commitment to preserving the world's forests while making beautiful and simple sustainable wooden furniture.
www.woodloops.de

### Bois stool,
### Cristian Mohaded

The multi-hued and patterned stripes of the Bois stool are a result of Cristian Mohaded's use of random scraps of abandoned wood. This technique not only reduces waste but also exploits the many different varieties, colours and grains of his chosen material.
www.mosch.com.ar

## Favela armchair, Fernando and Humberto Campana, Edra

Each of Edra's Favela chairs are built from off-cuts of waste pine – the same material used to build shanty towns in Brazil – and nailed together by hand. As a result, each chair is slightly different from the next, like the townships from which the chair draws its name.
www.edra.com

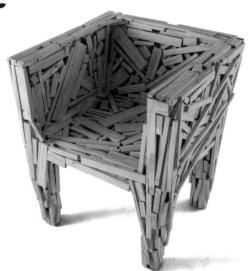

## Weidmann chair, Erika Hanson and Emiliano Godoy, Godoylab

The Weidmann chair is constructed from Maplex®, a next-generation material made from 100 percent wood fibres with no binders. The material readily accepts paints, dyes, stains and many adhesives and is 100 percent biodegradable and recyclable.
www.godoylab.com

## Carre stool, Inoda + Sveje, Conde House

With a combination of curved and straight lines, Carre uses approved wood and strict certified production methods to ensure that the ecological footprint of this stool is kept to a minimum. The wood frame also features a natural, no-toxin finish, while the seat is made of hemp.
www.condehouse.com

## Grandma's Bed stool, Claire Heather Danthois

Claire Heather Danthois creates sculptural and functional furniture using recycled timber – in this case, her Grandma's old bed. The curve of the stool is created using a steel cable, thereby eliminating the use of glue or toxins. It is also left free from paint or unnecessary finishes, another possible source of pollution.
www.coroflot.com

## Colombo chair, Matthew Hilton

Matthew Hilton's Colombo chair is constructed from sustainably sourced American black walnut or American white oak.
www.matthewhilton.com

## Angled Plywood Chair, Emiliano Godoy, Godoylab

The Angled Plywood Chair is made from lightweight FSC certified maple and walnut plywood, ergonomically curved and angled to release pressure normally placed on the user's bones when sitting, and to provide comfort without the need for synthetic cushioning. In addition, it is easy to manufacture, with no need for compound curve-bending or expensive tooling.
www.godoylab.com

## Fin dining chair, Matthew Hilton

Matthew Hilton's Fin dining chair is constructed from sustainably sourced American black walnut or American white oak.
www.matthewhilton.com

## Acorn Chair, Jonathan Tibbs

A beautifully simple oak chair with a slatted seat, the Acorn Chair is constructed from locally sourced sustainable oak and finished with natural, non-toxic oil.
www.jonathantibbs.com

## Latten Stuhl stackable chair, Max Gumpp and Hannes Gumpp

Using unfinished waste wood from construction sites, Max and Hannes Gumpp have created a very simple, stackable and lightweight chair. The minimalist structure is reduced to rectangular cuts, making the manufacturing process of the chair as straightfoward as possible.
www.hannesgumpp.com

### Udine chair,
### Lorenzo Damiani

The softwood used to create the Udine seat is made from recycled sawdust, discarded from other work projects. The chair can also be completely disassembled and recycled at the end of its life.
www.lorenzodamiani.net

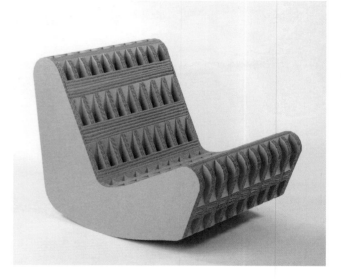

### Pool chair,
### Giles Miller, Farm Designs

Known as the 'King of Cardboard', Giles Miller's furniture is made from either recycled corrugated cardboard or with board from sustainably managed forests. The Pool chair is a classic example of his intelligent designs.
www.farmdesigns.co.uk

### Lisboa upholstered chair,
### Rita Burmester, Indoflex

Made from 30 percent natural fibres and 70 percent recycled foam, Rita Burmester turns traditional upholstery on its head by neglecting to cover the form of this usually concealed foam.
www.indoflex.com

## Lady 1 chair,
## Generoso Design

Constructed from a single sheet of double-corrugated cardboard, the Lady 1 chair is incredibly easy to assemble, and also folds away to facilitate transportation or storage.
www.generosodesign.it

## Banco bench,
## Woodloops

German design company Woodloops makes beautiful, simple furniture out of wood, exploiting the inherent qualities of the material. All wood used in the Banco bench is FSC certified and finished simply with natural oils.
www.woodloops.de

## Raw bench,
## Jason Iftakhar

Inspired by the possibilities of a supermarket baling machine, Jason Iftakhar designed the Raw bench in response to the huge amount of waste created by the food industry. The bench successfully promotes multiple lifecycles of industrial waste cardboard with minimal investment in energy.
www.jasoniftakhar.com

## Imprint chair, Johannes Foersom and Peter Hiort-Lorenzen, Lammhults

The Imprint chair is created from a radical new material called Cellupress, specially developed by Lammhults. A laminated wood-fibre mat material, it consists of compressed layers of recycled spruce, coconut and bark fibre, forming a thin and light textured wood material.
www.lammhults.se

## Soft Seating, Molo

Soft is a collection of seating, utilizing a honeycomb structure that fans open into stools, benches and loungers. Not intended to be disposable, the recycled and unbleached brown craft-paper surface improves with age, as its texture softens into a pleasing patina.
www.molodesign.com

## Motley, Samuel Chan, Channels

Recycled from cedar off-cuts, fused together to make a solid block and then turned on a giant lathe, Motley's drum-like forms can be used as seats or tables. They can also move between indoor and outdoor spaces, with the distinctive spicy aroma of cedar acting as a natural insect repellent.
www.channelsdesign.com

### PS Ellen rocking chair,
### Chris Martin, Ikea

Designed for everyone who was ever told off for leaning back on their chair at school, the PS Ellen rocking chair encourages the sitter to lean back and relax on its recycled and recyclable legs.
www.ikea.com

### Felt seat,
### Celia Suzanne Sluijter

Forming part of Celia Suzanne Sluijter's 'XO+' collection, the felt seat is made by women in Nepal under fairtrade conditions.
www.celia.nl

### Corky Lips armchair,
### Neo Design

A truly renewable resource, the manufacturing process of cork produces a near-zero wastestream and results in no toxic emissions. Constructed from recyclable foam and an innovative new cork-leather material, Neo Design's Corky Lips fully exploits the natural material's characteristics.
www.neodesignfurniture.com

### Brio chair, Mikiya Kobayashi

Offering a delicate update to the common wicker chair, the Brio illustrates a restrained use of rattan combined with an upholstered light steel frame.
www.mikiyakobashi.com

### Primo easy chair, Yngve Ekström, Swedese

The Primo easy chair, with its high or low back, has a laminated sustainable beech or oak veneer and is awarded the Nordic Swan eco-label. Products with this label must use traceable materials from sustainable sources and be manufactured without toxins.
www.swedese.se

### Holcim ottoman, Wyssem and Cecile Nochi

Part product design and part conceptual art, Holcim was created as part of a series of work highlighting the political situation in Lebanon. Holcim is constructed from used concrete sacks, refilled to create comfortable seats, and poses the question: 'Does anyone have any concrete ideas?'
www.wyssemnochi.com

## Reee Chair,
## Sprout Design Ltd, Pli Design

Made from recycled Sony PlayStations, the message cunningly placed at the back of the Reee Chair aims to make the user 'recycle again… and again… and again'. All the components of the Reee Chair – which diverts a remarkable 2,300 used plastic Sony PlayStation casings per chair from landfill – can easily be replaced and recycled.
www.plidesign.co.uk

## Super Elastica chair,
## Marco Zanuso and Giuseppe
## Rabori, Vittorio Bonacina

While recalling classic 1970's Vittorio Bonacina chairs, Marco Zanuso and Giuseppe Rabori's playful interpretation of the classic rattan chair also creates a totally contemporary look.
www.bonacinavittorio.it

## Flytip Chair,
## Alexena Cayless,
## Farm Designs

Alexena Cayless rescues discarded furniture from flytips and skips, reinventing them with a lick of fresh paint and graphic stencilling. Once completed, her pieces draw attention to the way once-loved items can be so casually abandoned.
www.farmdesigns.co.uk

### Adam and Eve chair, Ninette van Kamp and Rebecca Otero

A highly symbolic piece, the Adam and Eve chair is constructed from recycled furniture, textiles and ceramic. Unwanted pieces of furniture are transformed by the designer's use of plaster mixed with lace.
www.rebeccaotero.com

### Ottoman, Skoura

Constructed in Morocco in a fairtrade environment, this ottoman is made entirely from recycled car tyres.
www.skoura.co.uk

### Lamino chair, Yngve Ekström, Swedese

Voted 'the twentieth century's best Swedish furniture design', Yngve Ekström's Lamino chair features a laminated sustainable beech, oak, cherry or walnut veneer with sheepskin upholstery, and has also been awarded the Nordic Swan eco-label.
www.swedese.se

## Delucchi chair, Alberto Meda and Michele De Lucchi, Next Maruni

Constructed from sustainably sourced American maple, the Delucchi chair is finished in an environmentally friendly coating created by German company Auro. Free from any petroleum-derived ingredients, the coating is made from only natural and organic materials.
www.nextmaruni.com

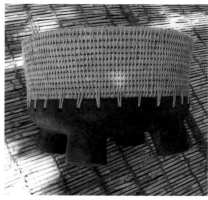

## Basket Stool, Rob van Acker

Together with the local craftspeople of Mongu, Zambia, Rob van Acker designed and created the Basket Stool from locally sourced materials.
www.robvanacker.com

## Eva chair, Giovanni Travasa, Vittorio Bonacina

Using sustainable rattan, this classic chair is woven by hand and is fully recyclable and biodegradable.
www.bonacina vittorio.it

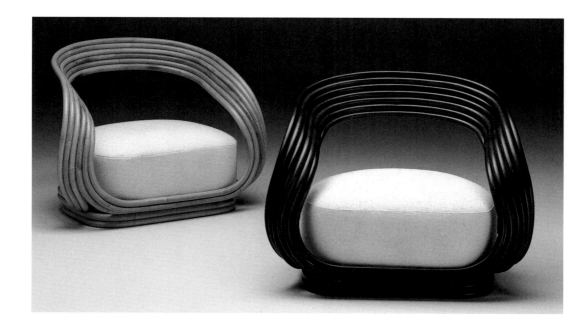

## Bourke's Luck chair, Ryan Frank

Built from the waste wood of old office desks, the Bourke's Luck chair comprises a sandwich of different woods layered together. Salvaged materials make up approximately 60–70 percent of the product's composition, while the remaining material is FSC certified plywood, required to provide necessary structural strength.
www.ryanfrank.net

## Harvey rocking stool, Ryan Frank

Built from old office desks, the Harvey stool comprises a mix of several different woods layered together, as in the Bourke's Luck chair above.
www.ryanfrank.net

## Twig bench, Russell Pinch, Pinch

Inspired by the simple concept of a bale of wood, the Twig bench comprises a plywood frame covered in dark muslin rather than paint, with coppiced hazel or willow added layer by layer and pinned together with hidden steel nails. The whole piece is sourced and made within a four-mile area, limiting transportation miles.
www.pinchdesign.com

## Shattered,
## Brent Comber

Shattered, created from sustainably sourced douglas fir, was inspired primarily by process. The designer was curious to see if he could create random patterns by splitting, assembling and juxtaposing different sizes, shapes and grain patterns of wood, and whether human nature would compel him to create order out of such chaos.
www.brentcomber.com

## Process Chair,
## Scott Garcia

Commenting that 'most people look at a steak and think of it with chips rather than legs,' Scott Garcia aims to raise consumer awareness of the origins of the products they use. The Process Chair, constructed from fallen sycamore, illustrates this point beautifully as the chair appears to grow out of the branch that forms its leg.
www.scottgarcia.moonfruit.com

## Accord chair,
## Lasse Pettersson,
## Lennart Notman,
## Skala Design,
## Swedese

Credited with the Nordic Swan eco-label, the Accord chair features a traceable birch or oak frame made from sustainable sources. In addition, no toxins are used in the manufacture of the chair and at the end of its life it is fully recyclable or biodegradable.
www.swedese.se

## 404 chair,
## Stefan Diez, Thonet

Inspired by Thonet's classic bentwood chairs, the 404 flows from a simple design idea: six pieces of curved wood form the legs and back support, joining together in a 'knot' underneath the centre of a reinforced seat. The wood is sourced entirely from controlled plantations and finished with a water-based, environmentally friendly lacquer.
www.thonet.com

## Spair chair,
## David Cameron and
## Toby Hadden, &Made

Offering an energy-efficient solution to seating, the Spair chair, constructed from sustainable birch plywood, is stored and transported flat to minimize its carbon footprint.
www.and-made.com

## Zaishu flat-
## packed chair,
## Matt Butler

Zaishu is a simply constructed, slot-together, flat-packed seat made from sustainable wood and water-based inks. Each one is unique, featuring one-off artworks or prints by Bollywood artists, Rangoli designers and Hindi signwriters. All proceeds go to support children in care.
www.dhub.org

## Gap chair,
## Studio
## Aisslinger

With a simple design based on a monoshape structure with a supporting cross under the seat, the ergonomic and minimalist proportions of the Gap chair reduce the need for materials, which results in a light, basic but elegant chair.
www.aisslinger.de

## Slot Chair,
## Raw Studio

Flat-packing significantly reduces a product's carbon footprint, a quality which Raw Studio wholeheartedly embraces in the Slot Chair. Produced from FSC certified materials, the chair is shipped unassembled, with instructions for various different configurations, leaving the user to slot it together as desired.
www.rawstudio.co.uk

## Bastian easy chair
## and ottoman,
## Robert A. Wettstein

Using a construction technique similar to making the wing of a glider, the Bastian easy chair and ottoman is made from an FSC certified wooden frame covered with wrapping paper. The product is extremely lightweight as it has a hollow core and is upholstered in paper.
www.wettstein.us

## Tapas chair, Matthew Hilton

The Tapas chair is a light, high-backed, three-legged dining chair constructed from sustainably sourced materials.
www.matthewhilton.com

## Gubi II chair, Komplot, Gubi

Made from a felt-polyester fibre extracted from used plastic water bottles, the Gubi II offers great strength and easy maintenance. In one single process, two mats of the recycled felt are moulded around the frame, water-cut and pronounced ready to use.
www.gubi.dk

## Sweet chair, Lorenzo Damiani

Sold flat-packed, thus reducing the energy required for transportation, Sweet uses a single sheet of Coverflex® material in an extremely functional and economical way. In addition, the chair can be disassembled and recycled at the end of its life.
www.lorenzodamiani.net

### Celle work chair, Jerome Caruso, Herman Miller

Developed using Herman Miller's cradle-to-cradle approach to design and the environment, the Celle work chair is constructed from a pliable polymer that is moulded into cells and loops. These flex and move with the sitter, ensuring properly distributed weight while working. Each part of the chair can be easily replaced, and is 99 percent recyclable.
www.hermanmiller.co.uk

### Think® chair, Steelcase

Described as 'the office chair with a brain and a conscience', the Think® chair is made from a minimum of materials, 41 percent of which are recycled. No PVC, chrome, mercury, lead or other toxic materials are used in the manufacturing process and, at the end of its long life, the chair is recyclable.
www.steelcase.com

### Retyred lounge chair, Jan Willem van Breugel, Wheels on Fire

Dutch designer Jan Willem van Breugel reuses abandoned bicycle parts found in his native Holland. With 16 million people in the country and nearly every one of them a cyclist, there are plenty of discarded tyres and parts. In the Retyred lounge chair, he has reupholstered the seat of a disused chair with woven tyre rubber.
www.wheels-on-fire.nl

## Fleece chair, Tom Price

Of all the plastic textiles, polyester is the most common. Some 11 million tonnes of polyester are produced each year. It is recyclable, although the recycling process releases toxic chemicals. Tom Price uses these unwanted fabrics to create his Fleece chairs. The chairs are not intended to offer a 'green' solution to issues surrounding the disposal of discarded plastics. Rather, Price hopes that his 'Meltdown Series', to which Fleece chair belongs, will help to elevate the status of plastic so that it is regarded as something to be cherished, appreciated and admired, rather than as something that is disposable and undesirable. This in turn, Price hopes, will ultimately result in less waste.
www.tom-price.com

## Réanim, 5.5 designers

Like a hospital for damaged furniture, Réanim repairs broken forms with contrasting new pieces.
www.cinqcinq designers.com

## Rocky rocking chair, Guy Arzi

Seeking out obsolete cinema seating, Guy Arzi restores, repaints and upholsters the original frames to create handmade, individual and distinct rocking chairs.
www.guyarzi.com

### Isabella seating, Ryan Frank

Inspired by hand-carved African designs, Ryan Frank's Isabella stool provides ergonomic seating in addition to a sculptural storage solution. Rather than using the exotic hardwoods featured in traditional African seating, the designer chose to work with 100 percent felted wool and strawboard – a sustainable, formaldehyde-free material made entirely from compressed straw. Strawboard is a durable material that offers a sustainable alternative to plasterboard and Frank's stools stand as a perfect example of the material's versatility.
www.ryanfrank.net

### Lost & Found Stool, &made

Constructed from a range of solid timbers and found furniture, &made's Lost & Found stools are available in a range of colours and styles.
www.and-made.com

### Balloon Back chair, Guy Arzi

Guy Arzi refurbishes antique furniture in contemporary fabrics and playful colour schemes. The Balloon Back chair is a classic example of his quirky refashioned antiques.
www.guyarzi.com

### Paper Mache armchair, Masif Designs

An experimental piece making effective use of waste materials, the Paper Mache armchair is built from inflatable chairs and used newspaper. Strengthened with cardboard, waste polystyrene, then several layers of newspaper, the chair is surprisingly strong and supportive.
www.masifdesigns.com

### Opuna Jasper chair and footstool, Startup, Start Up Design

The Opuna chair and footstool provides seating and comfort using only natural materials. Leather and rubberized hair are combined with sustainable Douglas fir to create a relaxing seat.
www.startupdesign.co.uk

### Makenge Armchair, Rob van Acker

Rob van Acker embraces the strong culture and craftsmanship of the Western Province of Zambia to produce fairtrade furniture. This seat is upholstered with the roots of the Makenge tree.
www.robvanacker.com

## High Stool, Peter Bundgaard Rützou and Signe Bindslev Henriksen, Mater

A high stool for occasional use, handcrafted in dark-stained FSC certified Chinese oak and black vegetable-tanned leather. This piece is produced at a small Chinese carpentry workshop in a fairtrade environment.
www.materdesign.com

## Guaiuba chair, Carlos Motta

The beaches of Brazil provide the inspiration behind designer Carlos Motta's sustainable designs. All his products are created from locally sourced, reused and recycled materials. The Guaiuba chair is no exception, and is created from reused cumaru wood sourced from the designer's native city of São Paolo.
www.carlosmotta.com.br

## Medium Saddle, Brent Comber

Designed for use inside and out, Brent Comber's Medium Saddle is carved from sustainable western red cedar and finished with a non-toxic hardwax oil.
www.brentccmber.com

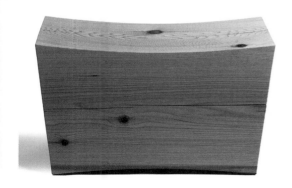

### Banca bench, Eugenio Menjivar

Eugenio Menjivar spent two years working as a design consultant for the USAID and NGO programme, Aid to Artisans, during which time he became aware that one of the main flaws with Brazilian design production – the lack of raw materials – could be solved with one of the country's main problems: trash. He now creates designs, like this bench, which make use of disused and unwanted materials.
www.eugeniomenjivar.com

### Eco Sofa, Retur Furniture, Nigel's Eco Store

Swedish based design company Retur produce furniture from cardboard, without sacrificing aesthetics or functionality. This eco-friendly sofa is made from 40 percent recycled sustainable cardboard, and is completely biodegradable.
www.nigelsecostore.com

### Ex Box Bench, Giles Miller

Built on a grid system for strength and versatility, the Ex Box Bench can be as narrow as a dining chair but can also be expanded infinitely by adding any number of Giles Miller's recycled corrugated cardboard sections.
www.gilesmiller.com

## Bump sofa, Remy Veenhuizen

The Bump sofa was commissioned for the digital depot of the Boymans van Beuningen Museum in Rotterdam. Not only do the hundreds of reused tennis balls represent the designer's intended theme of cell division, but they also provide an extremely comfortable and ready-upholstered building block.
www.remy veenhuizen.com

## Hump Bench, El Ultimo Grito

A simple p ne structure covered entirely in locally found discarded packing materials, the Hump Bench resembles an organic form despite its reuse of environmentally unfriendly ingredients of polystyrene, bubble wrap and packing tape.
www.elultimogrito.co.uk

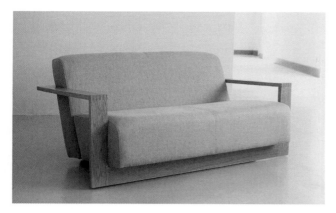

### Alvis Sofa,
### Terence Conran, Benchmark

Made from FSC certified comb-jointed oak, the geometric Alvis sofa has a traditional sprung seat and comes upholstered in either natural linen or the fabric of your choice.
www.benchmark-furniture.com

### Cushionized sofa,
### Christiane Hoegner

Comprising a solid ash framework and 40 separate pillows resembling a paintbox, the Cushionized sofa is ever-changing. Each infinitely adjustable cushion is filled with biodegradable, organically cultivated millet husks dipped in natural rubber.
www.christianehoegner.com

### Fern sofa,
### Marks & Spencer

Upholstered in fairtrade certified cotton covering a sustainable timber frame, each Fern sofa is filled with a combination of Ecoflex castor oil-based foam and fibre containing 122 plastic drinks bottles.
www.marksandspencer.com

### Lionel's Sofa, Squint

Typical of Squint's approach to design, Lionel's Sofa is a reclaimed Victorian Chesterfield, reupholstered with reused scraps of silk, cotton, velvet and ticking.
www.squintlimited.com

### Street Sofa, WEmake

The Street Sofa by WEmake gives retired Eurobins a more relaxing role in society. Cleverly cut and welded into shape, the sofa retains the original wheels and useful handles.
www.wemake.co.uk

### Max sofa, Reestore

Max the bath tub chaise. A contemporary twist on the sofa briefly featured in Breakfast at Tiffany's. Created from a vintage cast iron roll-top bath.
www.reestore.com

## Mercé bed, Woodloops

Celebrating the warmth and character of timber, the Mercé from Woodloops is a simple and robust design, available in FSC certified oak or cherry.
www.woodloops.de

## Shaker bed, Warren Evans

Having always sourced woods from responsibly managed supplies, Warren Evans now has the enviable distinction of being the UK's only FSC certified specialist bed-maker. In addition, his products are shipped in blankets for protection, rather than disposable plastic packaging.
www.warrenevans.com

## Maria bed, Woodloops

Woodloops make use of the natural strength and beauty of wood, while being actively committed to saving the world's forests. The Maria bed is handmade in Germany from FSC certified timber and left in its natural state, with any small cracks or blemishes accepted as part of the beauty of the material.
www.woodloops.de

### Tubed bed, Massimo Duroni

Identifying a cheap and strong building technique by lashing together discarded cardboard cylinders, Massimo Duroni's Tubed bed is assembled without screws or glue. It can also be easily dismantled in a few minutes.
www.arteda mangiare.it

### Makenge bed, Rob Van Acker

Typical of the designs from his 'Made in Mongu' label, Rob Van Acker's Makenge bed employs the unique skills and materials found in Zambia's Western Province, making use of local weavers to finish a frame of indigenous hardwood.
www.robvanacker.com

### GallopyGallopy bed, Charlie Whinney

Looking like it might suddenly bounce across the room, the GallopyGallopy is a well-named bed, combining sustainable timber slats with a steel frame mounted on reused springs.
www.charliewhinney.com

### Alfred bed, Sean Sutcliffe, Benchmark

A simplified, geometric version of the classic English four poster bed, Benchmark's Alfred bed comprises a base and frame of sustainable solid oak, with beech slats.
www.benchmark-furniture.com

### Mattresses, Abaca Organic

Made without synthetic materials or chemical additives, Abaca Organic's mattresses are upholstered in undyed, unbleached organic cotton and replace foam with organic Welsh sheep's wool and coconut fibres.
www.abacaorganic.co.uk

### Le Petit Voyage bed, Kenneth Cobonpue

A cosy cocoon of abaca vine and buri, Le Petit Voyage is made in the Philippines from natural fibres processed entirely without machinery. The fibres are then secured to a frame of recycled metal with abaca rope, considered to be the strongest natural fibre in the world.
www.kenneth cobonpue.com

### Muir bed, Nicole Chaila, Amenity Home

Conscientiously made by local artisans from solid, reclaimed Douglas Fir and finished only with low VOC, water-based materials, Amenity Home's Muir bed is a graceful complement to their natural bedding.
www.amenityhome.com

### Books modular system, Studio Aisslinger

Based on a simple cross-shaped metal connector, Aisslinger's design is an open-ended modular system, which assembles unused and outdated books, either as a shelving unit or simply as a constantly expanding display format.
www.aisslinger.de

### Matz CD storage unit, Woodloops

Available in oiled FSC certified oak or cherry, Matz is a labyrinthine CD storage unit designed with a single swirling shelf that traces an angular line across the entire design.
www.woodloops.de

### MH024 Storage, Matthew Hilton

Available in sustainably sourced teak, paramara or mahogany, Matthew Hilton's geometric MH024 Storage comprises a rigid grid of shelving, offset by a decorative panel of more abstract linear designs.
www.matthewhilton.com

## On the Piss, Simon Mount, Doistrinta

Produced using FSC approved timbers, Simon Mount's On the Piss bookshelf is designed to last for generations.
www.thegreenhaus.co.uk

## Vagabond Cabinet of Curiosities, John D. O'Leary, BlueGreen&Co

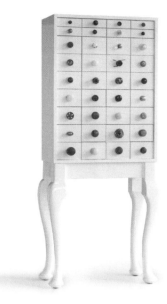

Vagabond originated from a series of photographs taken over a 12 month period of 'homeless' furniture thrown out on the streets of Edinburgh. Amazed at the quality of such 'rubbish', the designer began to collect wood and various materials from skips and garbage bins. The cabinet is an attempt to give value back to these materials, once disregarded as worthless junk. Inside, each drawer is unique, handcrafted from different reclaimed woods, including brown oak, sycamore, walnut, birch plywood, chipboard and pine. Each drawer knob is also different.
www.bluegreenandco.com

## Alinata shelving system, Satyendra Pakhalé

Alinata is a freestanding modular shelving system by Satyendra Pakhalé, comprising a futuristic framework of extruded recycled aluminium, contrasting with more traditional panels of glass or sustainable bamboo.
www.satyendra-pakhale.com

## Tree coatstand, Budi Joseph, Blaowww

Reasoning that design with simplicity and humour results in a world where there is more room for your imagination, Blaowww has created a recycled corrugated cardboard coatstand that resembles a tree.
www.blaowww.com

## Baobab coatstand, Xavier Lust, Mdf Italia

Made from Ekotek, an innovative, fully recyclable, polyester and mineral resin, Mdf Italia's Baobab is a unique sculptural coatstand, which recalls Africa's 'tree of life'.
www.mdfitalia.it

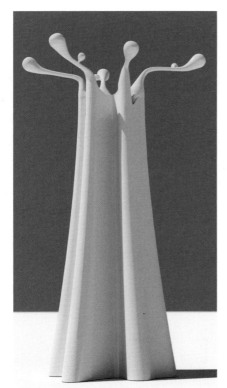

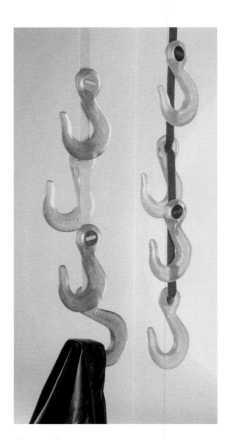

## Grapple storage system, Ryan Frank

A storage system designed for home or retail use, Grapple uses adjustable hooks made from 'bio-resin' – a natural, non-toxic plant-based material. These are attached to a length of hemp webbing with stainless steel buckles.
www.ryanfrank.net

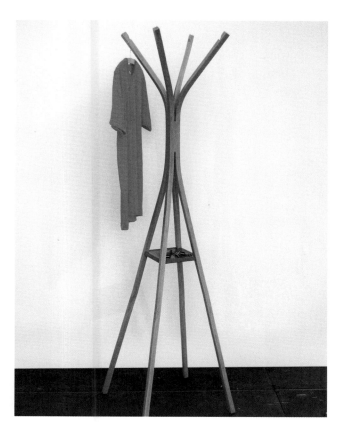

### Coatstand,
### David Sutton

The simple design of David Sutton's sustainable steam-bent oak coatstand employs square-cut timber that lends itself to a reduction in waste materials by eliminating off-cuts and the need for complicated shaping.
www.davidsutton.co.uk

### Lobby bench,
### Allan
### McIntyre,
### Bluegreen
### & co

Modern manufacturing techniques meet the heritage of the coastal communities near Fife in this beautiful and useful bench.
www.bluegreen andco.com

### Hallstand,
### Oliver Tilbury

Constructed from English oak, FSC certified birch plywood and 100 percent wool felt, Oliver Tilbury's hallstand is a response to the need for a hat stand, umbrella pot, place to sit and point of storage to be brought together in one solution.
www.olivertilbury.com

## Bookstack modular bookshelf, A4A Design

A4A Design's Bookstack is a modular bookshelf in recycled honeycombed cardboard, stackable up to four layers high and available in versatile configurations to fit specific situations.
www.a4adesign.it

## Eco Friendly Bookshelf, Nigel's Eco Store

A no-gimmicks, capacious storage unit, the Eco Friendly Bookshelf is made from sustainable recycled cardboard to a simple, smart and strong design.
www.nigelseco store.com

## Make/Shift storage and transportation system, Peter Marigold

The wedge-shaped sections of Make/Shift allow it to fit tightly into spaces between walls. The sustainable plywood units can be bolted together and used as crates for transporting goods.
www.petermarigold.com

## Rock 'n' Roll shelves, Retur Design

Rock'n'Roll is a unique shelving system made from unbleached high-density paperboard rolls. The rolls can be fixed together on installation in various configurations and are held in place by super-strong Velcro.
www.nigelsecostore.com

## Cesaria Evoria storage system, Godoylab

Cesaria Evoria is a clever method of recycling any number of empty steel cans into a useful storage system. To eliminate the need for transit, assembly instructions are available on the Godoylab website.
www.godoylab.com

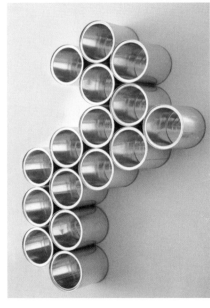

## SAK bookshelf, Godoylab

SAK is a bookshelf made from 12 identical flat-packed pieces of FSC certified birch, slotted together without fixings or adhesive and designed for biodegradation.
www.godoylab.com

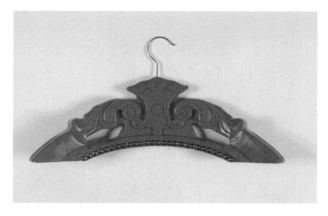

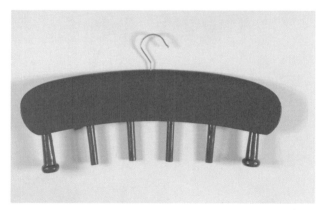

## Hanging Back coat hangers, Sebastien Hejna, Farm Designs

Perhaps acknowledging that it is always easier to hang clothes on a chair instead of on a hanger where they belong, Hanging Back by Sebastien Hejna uses the remains of discarded furniture to provide a pleasing compromise.
www.farmdesigns.co.uk

## Cityscape coat hangers, Sixixis

Fashioned from sustainable timber, Sixixis's Cityscape coat hangers fill an overlooked space with a choice of iconic skyline motifs.
www.sixixis.com

## Alba Armoire, Russel Pinch, Pinch

Pinch's beautiful Armoire collection is handmade by some of the UK's finest craftsmen. Each piece is built from sustainably sourced timbers and designed to last. Each Armoire is followed through the workshop by just one maker, is stamped with the maker's mark, then numbered and signed on completion. These versatile pieces are built to last and designed to be enjoyed for generations. www.pinch design.com

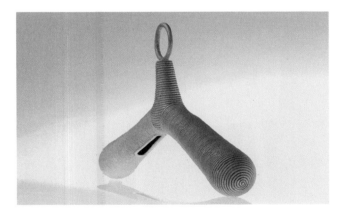

## Bell Metal Hanger, Satyendra Pakhalé

Made of recycled bronze, brass and copper alloy, the hanger is produced using an ancient method of metal casting. In our modern society this technique was largely abandoned as it was considered too costly because it requires too many hand-crafted-steps. www.satyendra-pakhale.com

## Zilka clothes hanger, Ryan Frank

Ryan Frank's Zilka is a clothes hanger made from recycled and repulped British newspapers. www.ryanfrank.net

## Cocktail cabinet, Jimmie Martin

This reused cocktail cabinet is transformed with splashes of vibrant colour.
www.jimmie martin.co.uk

## Reinvented Cabinet, Caroline Till

On an otherwise formal piece of discarded furniture, Caroline Till's Reinvented Cabinet hints at an irreverent approach with its bold, bright and hand-painted makeover, inspired by contrasts between contemporary and traditional design.
caroline@carolinetill.com

## Flytip Furniture Cabinet, Alexena Cayless

Rescued from landfill, Alexena Cayless' cabinet makes no secret of its past, emblazoned with an image of its teak-veneered previous incarnation.
www.farmdesigns.co.uk

## White Imperfection sideboard, Jimmie Martin

A reclaimed antique sideboard scrawled with graffiti and handwriting, Jimmie Martin's cabinet radically transforms a once conservative piece of furniture.
www.jimmiemartin.co.uk

## Bedside cabinet, Oliver van der Breggen

Intended to last for hundreds of years and crafted in FSC certified walnut or cherry, the angular and faceted appearance of this cabinet draws inspiration from mechanical forms.
ollyvdb@hotmail.com

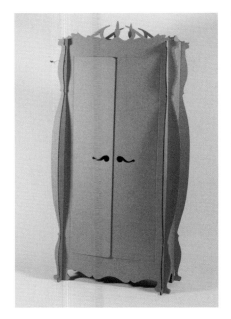

## Wardrobe-C, Giles Miller

Designed in the style of a rather more grand piece of furniture, Giles Miller's Wardrobe-C cleverly uses recycled corrugated cardboard, cut out and slotted together.
www.gilesmiller.com

## Drive-In Wardrobe, Florian Kräutli and Gaële Girault, Droog

A barely disguised pallet of sustainable bamboo provides the structure for Droog's Drive-In Wardrobe. Studded with magnets, the curtain concealing the interior can be hung in your own unique sculptural preference.
www.droog.com

## Hackney Shelf mobile shelving, Ryan Frank

The Hackney Shelf originated from white boards made of waste wood chips that were temptingly displayed around East London by Ryan Frank. The boards were inevitably covered in graffiti and then transformed into mobile shelving units.
www.ryanfrank.net

## Hackney Lite mobile shelving unit, Ryan Frank

Hackney Lite is a follow-up design to the Hackey Shelf, but with an undecorated white face, allowing the owner to do the graffiti in the privacy of their home.
www.ryanfrank.net

## White Rot sideboard, Derek Welsh

Made from sustainable Scottish sycamore with the distinctive spotted markings of white rot fungi, Derek Welsh's sideboard shows the influence of modernism and geometric forms on his design.
www.derekwelsh.co.uk

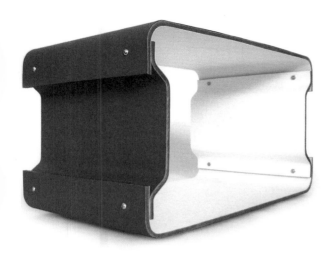

## Blue Shelf, Godoylab

Describing sustainability as 'the primary framework within which we develop products and projects', Godoylab's Blue Shelf is constructed from certified timbers with a non-toxic finish.
www.godoylab.com

## Flex shelf, Lorenzo Damiani, Montina

Designed with a cradle-to-cradle approach, Flex is constructed from sustainable wood and can be fully disassembled and recycled at the end of its life. The product is also flat-packed for transit to reduce its carbon footprint.
www.montina.it

## Quattrolibri mobile book and magazine holder, Raffaella Mangiarotti, Deepdesign, Coin

Deepdesign's Quattrolibri is a mobile book and magazine holder constructed from sustainable laminated bamboo. It may be placed vertically or used horizontally as a coffee table.
www.deepdesign.it
www.coin.it

## You Can't Lay Down Your Memory chest of drawers, Tejo Remy, Droog

A motley collection of salvaged drawers fitted into sustainable maple boxes and tied into a bundle with a jute strap, Tejo Remy's teetering chest of drawers is a perfect example of Droog's innovative approach to design.
www.droog.com

## Hey Chair! Be a Bookshelf, Maarten Baas

Saving discarded furniture from landfill, Maarten Baas' assemblages give unwanted objects unexpected new functions. In this way a chair can be a shelf (as here) or a violin may become a coat rack…
www.maartenbaas.com

## Legend collection shelf, Roche Bobois

This twig-like bookshelf, made from FSC certified French oak, is from the limited edition Legend collection by Roche Bobois.
www.roche-bobois.com

### Dugout Canoe Bookshelves, Rob van Acker

Combining weather-beaten aluminium panels from scrapped Land Rovers and leaky dugout canoes, Rob van Acker gives these retired workhorses a new incarnation as bookshelves with a palpable history.
www.robvanacker.com

### Land Rover Aluminium Drawers, Rob van Acker

Traditionally used by locals to make pots and pans, Rob van Acker takes aluminium from scrap Land Rovers in Zambia for a variety of projects including these folded and riveted drawers from his 'Made in Mongu' label.
www.robvanacker.com

### Lack shelf, Ikea

Despite their robust appearance, Ikea's Lack shelves have a board-on-frame hollow construction, filled with recycled paper, making them half the weight of solid shelves and therefore easier and more efficient to transport.
www.ikea.com

## Pedi mobile office storage, Simon Mount, Doistrinta

Made in FSC certified birch ply or walnut, Pedi is a mobile office storage cabinet with two detachable stools integrated into the design.
www.designfactory.org

## Pack of Dogs shelving, NEL Collective, Godoylab

Based on the shapes of dogs in different positions and named after famous Mexican wrestlers, this range of shelving is made using post-industrial off-cuts of FSC certified beech, maple and oak.
www.godoylab.com

## Wall Stool, Lorenzo Damiani

Made of recycled wood, Wall Stool is characterized by a double function: it can be used as either storage or a stool. In this way it also saves energy.
www.lorenzo damiani.net

## Tavola storage table, Rezzoli

Designed as a silent protest against the globalized furniture industry and a role-model for a local approach, Tavola by Rezzolli is handmade in Switzerland and employs traditional Engadin woodworking skills in an attempt to highlight the little-known characteristics of locally sourced, sustainable larch.
www.rezzoli.ch

## Decades cabinet, WIS Design

Offering a miniature history of twentieth-century furniture design, the Decades cabinet by WIS Design features a range of drawers salvaged from flea markets in a new, painted surround.
www.wisdesign.se

## Hylly shelf, Durat

Hylly shelf is constructed from contrasting colours of Durat, a solid polyester-based material containing recycled plastics. It is extremely durable and 100 percent recyclable.
www.durat.com

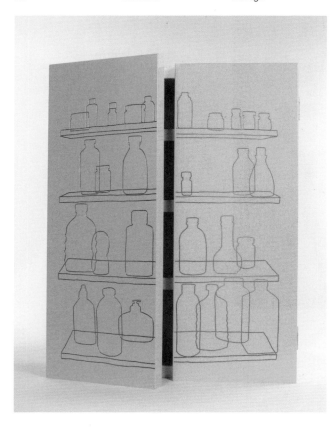

### Inside-Out cabinet, Freshwest

From their 'Inside-Out' range, Freshwest's cabinet is made from aluminium composite with a recycled plastic core.
www.freshwest.co.uk

### Soso cabinets, Patty Johnson, Mabeo

Mabeo is committed to the production of high end contemporary furniture in Botswana, Africa. The company's Soso cabinet is designed by Patty Johnson as part of her North South Project, which helps Southern hemisphere manufacturers find Northern hemisphere markets for their products.
www.mabeofurniture.com

### Colony Modular Storage, George Gold Furniture Design

George Gold produces a small range of batch production furniture made entirely from solid hardwood. The timber is harvested from managed sources in the UK, Europe and the US. The shelving is constructed to stand up to more than a lifetime of service, with the solid hardwood improving with age.
www.georgegoldfurnituredesign.co.uk

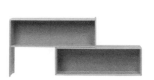

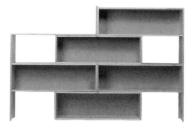

## Factum CD storage, Art Meets Matter

From their Factum range, Art Meets Matter's CD storage is folded and slotted from a single piece of flat, chintz-printed, 100 percent recycled paperboard.
www.artmeetsmatter.com

## Sideboard, Unto This Last

Made in FSC certified birch, Unto This Last's sideboards use no disposable packing materials and are wrapped in blankets for weekly delivery within London on an energy-saving, optimized route.
www.untothislast.co.uk

## Grass Cabinet, Pli Design

Despite its appearance, the Grass Cabinet contains no wood at all and in fact has a core of wheat strawboard, veneered with natural wax-coated bamboo. Apart from its recyclable aluminium legs, the cabinet is designed to be completely compostable and contains no chemicals.
www.plidesign.co.uk

## Clifton shelves, Terence Conran, Benchmark

Named for its resemblance to the iconic suspension bridge in Bristol, England, the Clifton is made in sustainable solid ash with traditional exposed joints, and held rigid by adjustable stainless steel wires.
www.benchmark-furniture.com

## Purmerend tallboy, Derek Welsh

This unique tallboy has five drawers made of locally sourced, sustainable Scottish walnut mounted on Derek Welsh's signature-style plinth.
www.derekwelsh.co.uk

## Object Deluxe storage boxes, Lago

Simultaneously mocking and questioning the idea of luxury with their ironic 'Object Deluxe' series, Lago reproduce the trappings of wealth and sophistication on recycled cardboard boxes.
www.lago.it

## Biblo modular shelving, Generoso Parmegiani

Designed as a bookcase or display stand, Generoso Parmegiani's Biblo is a recycled cardboard modular shelving system, which is infinitely expandable in width and stackable up to 2m (6ft) high.
www.generosodesign.it

## End Shelves modular storage system, Jasper Startup

Created from locally sourced scraps of waste timber, Jasper Startup's End Shelves are an infinitely expandable modular storage system.
www.startup design.co.uk

## Secretary, Evelien Valk

Based on a traditional desk but with a modern asymmetrical form, the Secretary is designed in reaction to the inefficient use of materials in the modern furniture industry and is made entirely from a single piece of sustainable oak, with no off-cuts.
www.evelienvalk.nl

# Lighting

### Nikau light, MOA, David Trubridge

Nikau is designed to use the minimum amount of material to maximum effect. The light is constructed from sustainably sourced plywood, the least wasteful form of timber conversion, and finished in non-toxic natural oils.
www.davidtrubridge.com

### Nautilus lampshade, Rebecca Asquith

The aptly named Nautilus by New Zealand designer Rebecca Asquith takes its shell-like form from GECA (Good Environment Choice Australia) certified hoop-pine plywood. It comes flat-packed in kit form, reducing packaging and making for efficient transportation.
www.rebeccaasquith.com

### Floral flat-packed lampshade, David Trubridge

A lamp of elemental simplicity, David Trubridge's Floral is flat-packed in a kit and assembled at home. The shade is constructed from sustainable, repeat-patterned CNC-cut plywood, resulting in minimum waste. It is finished with non-toxic natural oils.
www.davidtrubridge.com

## Punga flat-pack light, Christopher Metcalfe

Punga lights are inspired by a palm tree that abounds in designer Christopher Metcalfe's native New Zealand. Stripped of its bristle-like bark the tree reveals a beautiful pattern of cellular-like ovals. The lights are produced by laser cutting sustainably sourced Australian hoop pine; a process that results in extremely low waste. The product also ships extremely efficiently as a flat-pack.
www.christopher
metcalfe.com

## Koura hanging lamp, MOA, David Trubridge

Following David Trubridge's beautifully simple aesthetic, Koura is a hanging lamp constructed of either sustainable ash or hop-pine plywood and aluminium rivets.
www.davidtrubridge.com

## Light Reading chandelier, Lucy Jane Norman

This chandelier recycles unwanted books that would ordinarily have been thrown away. It is made by folding each page of a book in half, producing a circular arrangement that hangs around a ceiling light. A natural, non-toxic finish is applied to make the paper flame-retardant.
www.lucynorman.
co.uk

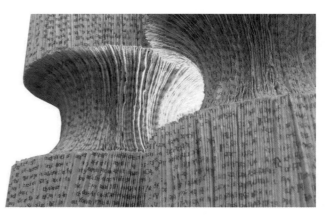

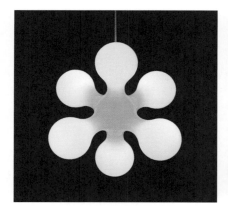

## Atomium lamp, Osko+Deichmann, Kundalini

Atomium is a suspension lamp, specifically designed to be illuminated with low-energy lightbulbs.
www.kundalini.it

## Lech chandelier, Isabel Hamm

Illuminated by just one low-energy halogen bulb, Lech is a chandelier of glass rods resembling a ball-shaped bunch of glass flowers. The light feeds from above and passes through to the end of each rod, illuminating the very tip of every flower.
www.isabel-hamm.de

## Cog light, Blue Marmalade

Blue Marmalade utilize recycled and recyclable material for all their products. They also adhere to a strict zero-landfill policy. The Cog is constructed from recyclable polypropylene and is designed to accept an energy-saving lightbulb. This light is also transported flat-packed for reduced packaging and maximum energy efficiency.
www.bluemarmalade.co.uk

## Saving Grace lamp, Adrien Rovero, Droog

Designed especially to take an energy-saving lightbulb, Droog's Saving Grace lamp, constructed from sandblasted glass, shows that energy-saving lamps can be beautiful too.
www.droog.com

## Other People's Rubbish lampshade, Heath Nash

Heath Nash's delicate work demonstrates the possibility of taking reused discarded plastic to a sophisticated level.
www.heathnash.com

## Bloom flat-pack light, Blue Marmalade

The Bloom light has an organic form inspired by flowers and seashells, and is specifically designed for use with an energy-saving lightbulb. The light is constructed from recyclable polypropylene and is transported flat-packed to reduce waste and maximize efficiency.
www.bluemarmalade.co.uk

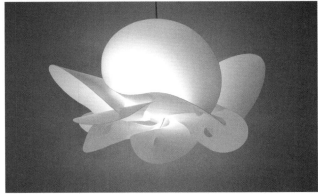

## Soft Crack II lamp, Massimiliano Adami

This eyecatching pendant lamp is created using recycled broken ceramics.
Massi.adami@tin.it

### Vintage lampshades, Kathleen Hills

Playing with our nostalgia for the past, by reinterpreting the familiar and placing it in a contemporary setting, Kathleen Hills' Vintage pendants are produced from reclaimed glass shades, rescued from bric-à-brac shops and skips. Additional parts include modern bone china fittings, manufactured by a local family-run company, energy-saving bulbs and recycled packaging.
www.kathleenhills.co.uk

### Spectacle chandelier, Stuart Haygarth

Spectacle is created from 1020 pairs of disused prescription spectacles. By using prescriptive spectacles, another aid to seeing, an interesting analogous line is drawn between their old and new purposes.
www.stuarthaygarth. com

### Tide chandelier, Stuart Haygarth

The original Tide chandelier is part of a larger body of work based on the collection of manmade debris washed up on the Kent coastline. The chandelier is created from clear and translucent objects, primarily made of plastic. Each object is different in shape and form, yet together they produce one sphere.
www.stuarthaygarth.com

## Milk Bottle Lamp, Tejo Remy, Droog

Tejo Remy's Milk Bottle Lamp consists of 12 recycled milk bottles. Each bottle is sandblasted and fitted with a stainless steel ceiling cap and low-energy bulb, then hung like a milk bottle crate, in a grid just above the floor.
www.droog.com

## Pegasus reading light, Antoinet Deurloo and Michael Bom, Atelier Bom Design

A clever and innovative take on a traditional reading light, Atelier Bom Design turns used books into elegant lighting features that emit a soft glow.
www.bomdesign.nl

## Capsule light, Jaime Salm and Katherine Wise, Mio

Made from two capsule-like felt shells – one in colour to direct light and the other in white to diffuse it – Mio's Capsule pendant lamp emits a soft and relaxing glow. It is designed for use with a low-energy bulb and can be easily dissembled for transportation and recycling.
www.mioculture.com

### Drunk, Yoon Bahk

Yoon Bahk's Drunk is a cluster of glass wine bottles which have been sliced through, sandblasted, and illuminated with super-bright LEDs.
www.yoonbahk.com

### Orbita Light, Tomoko Mizu, Vittorio Bonacina

Sustainable rattan is used to produce the elegant curves of Vittorio Bonacina's Orbita light.
www.bonacina vittorio.it

### Cascade, Michelle Brand

Made from reused plastic bottles, Michelle Brand's Cascade is a pendant light, which falls from ceiling to floor, creating an iconic and dramatic focal point.
www.michellebrand.co.uk

### Ribbon, Tom Raffield, MARK

Tom Raffield makes each of these large feature pendant lights using traditional steam-bending techniques. Each has a unique signature of looping sustainable ash or oak, illuminated by a compact low-energy lamp.
www.markproduct.com

## Ash Pendant, Tom Raffield

Tom Raffield's Ash Pendant lamps feature a delicate steam-bent shade constructed entirely from locally sourced strips of FSC certified English ash.
www.tomraffield.com

## Curly lampshade, Charlie Whinney

Steam-bent sustainable ash coils, twists and winds around a central steam-bent ash frame to make Charlie Whinney's Curly shade. Each one is a unique piece and is signed and numbered by the designer.
www.charliewhinney.com

## 3star light, David Henrichs, DH Product Design

The modern futuristic lines of David Henrich's 3Star light are specifically designed to take energy-saving bulbs.
www.hiddenart london.co.uk

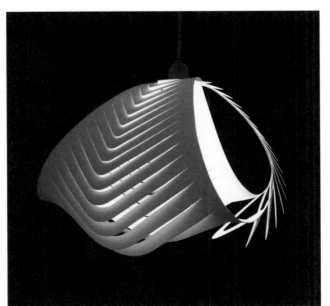

## Soft Crack light, Massimiliano Adami

Massimiliano Adami recycles broken ceramics in this eco-sensitive design.
Massi.adami@tin.it

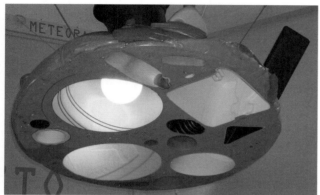

## Meteora light, Massimiliano Adami

Using a plethora of recycled containers and coloured polyurethane foam, Massimiliano Adami produces imaginative recycled lights that look as if they might have fallen from outer space.
Massi.adami@tin.it

## Dark Side of Bikini chandelier, Regis-R

Regis-R transforms an assortment of discarded rubbish into a chandelier in Dark Side of Bikini.
r.egis.online.fr

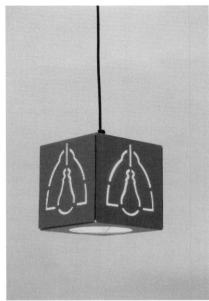

## Not a Box lampshade, David Graas

David Graas is committed to designing products that can easily be reused or recycled. Not a Box integrates packaging and product into one. The cut-out of the lamp shape hints at its use while all necessary parts (bulb, cable and lamp holder) are inside with a small manual for installation.
www.davidgraas.com

## Tree lampshade, Simon Mount and Laura Baxter, Doistrinta

Doistrinta embrace the warm, tactile qualities of cork in their Tree lampshades. Harvested by hand from the bark of the cork oak tree in an undamaging nine-year cycle, cork is recyclable, impermeable and totally sustainable.
www.designfactory.org

## Flute pendant, Giles Miller

Giles Miller produces the innovative and visually stunning Flute pendant from either recycled or sustainably managed corrugated cardboard. Each floral pattern is hand-fluted into the surface of the card, creating a unique, eco-sensitive shade.
www.gilesmiller.com

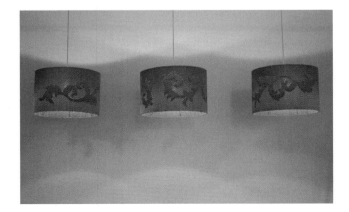

### Fish Trap lampshade, Rob van Acker

Illustrating that almost any disused vessel can be transformed into a lampshade, Rob van Acker uses disused fish traps from the Mongu region to create simple and sustainable lampshades.
www.robvanacker.com

### Woven lampshade, Rob van Acker

As part of Rob van Acker's 'Made in Mongu' series, the designer works with local craftsmen to produce tactile lamps made with a combination of ceramics and weaving.
www.robvanacker.com

### Wai Wai Weavers lights, Patty Johnson, North South Project

Part of Patty Johnson's North South Project, these lights are produced in collaboration with the Wai Wai Weavers of Guyana, South America. The project is a fairtrade design and craft collaboration aimed at improving the economical, cultural and ecological environment in which the products are produced.
www.northsouthproject.com

## Miss Light lampshade, Jasper Startup

The Miss Light is constructed from sustainably sourced birch plywood and is designed for use with an energy-saving bulb.
www.startupdesign.co.uk

## Lampshades, Rachel Bending, Bird

Recognised as Australia's first climate-neutral business in 2004, Bird products are made using solar powered and low-impact local production methods. Bird also offset any carbon emissions created by their business. The hand-drawn botanical designs on their drum shades are hand-printed using water-based dyes on natural organic fabric
www.birdtextile.com.au

## Bell Light, Jasper Startup, Gervasoni

Woven from 100 percent natural sustainable materials and designed to take an energy-saving lightbulb, the Bell Light provides a simple and honest solution to eco-sensitive lighting.
www.gervasoni1882.it

## Bendant Lamp, Jaime Salm, Katherine Wise, Mio

The Bendant Lamp is a flat-packed chandelier composed of a series of laser-cut, leaf-like shades surrounding a central fixture. The size of the lamp, shape of the cuts and flat packaging are all designed for maximum material efficiency. In addition, the leaf-like shades can be selectively bent to achieve unique light and shadow compositions.
www.mioculture.com

## Coron lamp, Mixko

Made from 100 percent sustainable wool felt and featuring a simple button or snap near its base, Coron takes an energy-saving lightbulb.
www.mixko.co.uk

## Shadey lamp, Lisa Widén and Anna Irinarchos, WIS Design

A collection of old, unwanted lampshades piled on each other, Shadey is a pendant lamp with an unusual yet familiar appearance.
www.wisdesign.se

## Shadey Family chandelier, Stuart Haygarth

A linear chandelier created from a selection of found glass lampshades, Shadey Family recycles unwanted and discarded lampshades and reconfigures them to create a harmonious entity.
www.stuarthaygarth.com

## Other People's Rubbish chandelier, Heath Nash

Heath Nash draws on his local South African craft tradition of using recycled plastic bottles and other objects to make something entirely new; in this case, a chandelier.
www.heathnash.com

## Straight Lamp, Jan Willem van Breugel, Wheels on Fire

Dutch designer Jan Willem van Breugel collects old, broken and abandoned bicycles and transforms them into new products. This chandelier is recycled from a disused bicycle wheel.
www.wheels-on-fire.nl

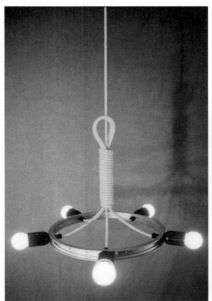

## Disposable Chandelier, Stuart Haygarth

Created from 416 disposable plastic wine glasses illuminated with a pink fluorescent light, Stuart Haygarth's Disposable Chandelier gives permanence to throwaway items.
www.stuarthaygarth.com

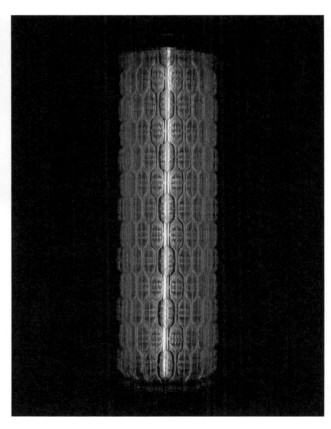

### Chandelier, Demelza Hill

Made from recycled shot glasses, this piece is inspired by the waste of plastic drinking containers at events and parties.
www.demelzahill.com

### Swarth Light, Rethink Things

A lamp shade made entirely from post-industrial aluminium waste, Swarth reflects and refracts light in a chaotic explosion.
www.rethinkthings.co.uk

### Come Rain Come Shine chandelier, Tord Boontje, Artecnica

Artecnica's 'Design With Conscience' projects aim to create products in accordance with humanitarian and environmentally friendly principles. Come Rain Come Shine is Tord Boontje's lyrical reinvention of the traditional chandelier, with crocheted cotton, organza and silk flowers gracefully surrounding a solid metal base. It is handcrafted in collaboration with Brazil's Coopa-Roca Women's Cooperative.
www.artecnicainc.com

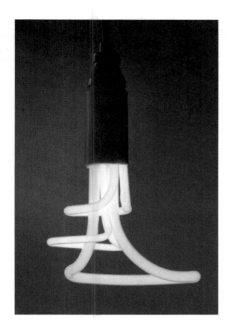

## Plumen light, Hulger

Hulger's decorative low-energy lightbulb is a reaction to standard lightbulbs, which are usually considered to need to be covered.
www.hulger.com

## Cut Glasses chandelier, John Harrington

The Cut Glasses chandelier is constructed from a vast collection of discarded cut crystal glasses. The stunning chandelier is suspended from an illuminated, cast glass ceiling rose.
www.johnharrington design.com

## Quentin Lampshade, Hamid Van Koten and Ian Carnduff

Manufactured from recycled paper-mill waste, which is vacuum-drawn through a porous mould, Quentin was designed with the aim of producing a durable, recycled product using a low-energy, high-speed production process.
h.h.vankoten@dundee.ac.uk

## Solid light, Nina Tolstrup, Studiomama

Designed using salvaged wood and a low-energy bulb, Solid is a simple and sustainable wall light.
www.studiomama.com

## Luce lighting feature, Antoinet Deurloo and Michael Bom, Atelier Bom Design

A clever and innovative take on a reading light, Atelier Bom Design hand-craft used books into softly glowing lighting features.
www.bomdesign.nl

## Bianca lamp, Lorenzo Damiani and Tiziano Bono

Bianca is a low-energy wall lamp that also functions as a portable energy socket. The lamp features a socket to charge a mobile phone or laptop and can easily be detached and moved elsewhere in the house.
www.lorenzo damiani.net

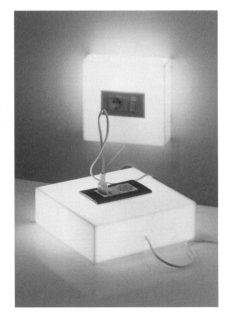

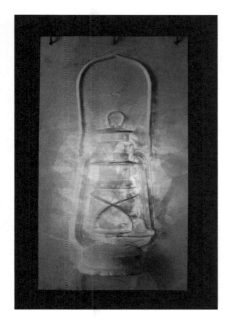

## Lanternsconce,
## Harry Allen, Areaware

Forming part of the 'Reality' series, which consists of objects whose form is 'sampled' from existing sources, the Lantern sconce is made of ricepaper and glue.
www.areaware.com

## Fingers Crossed wall light, Partridge & Walmsley, Benchmark

Fingers Crossed is a wall light constructed from two pieces of sustainable oak, sliced at the ends and slotted into each other. The light also features a recyclable aluminium shade.
www.benchmark-furniture.com

## Clutch Light,
## Scott Jarvie

Scott Jarvie seeks to reduce material wastage with this design made from 10,000 reclaimed drinking straws.
www.scottjarvie.co.uk

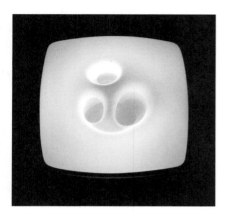

### Alone lamp,
### Giorgio Gurioli,
### Kundalini

Alone is a low-energy wall and ceiling lamp with a diffusing Plexiglas frame.
www.kundalini.it

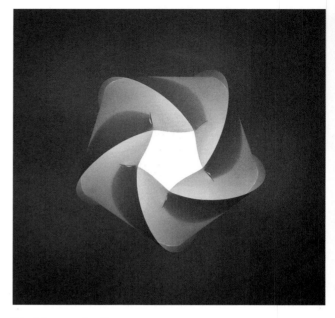

### Bud lampshade,
### Blue Marmalade

Designed to accept almost all energy saver lightbulbs, Bud is a pendant lampshade designed to promote the use of energy-saving bulbs. The light is supplied flat-packed.
www.bluemarmalade.co.uk

### Radiance light,
### Edward Horsford

Where multiple lights in a room can often call for long banks of switches, Edward Horsford's Radiance aims to provide a new interface for users to control their lighting in a more natural and usable manner. The light is designed using a low-energy light source.
www.edwardhorsford.com

## Bailarina, Eugenio Menjivar

Salvadoran designer Eugenio Menjivar creates repurposed lamps made from egg cartons.
www.eugenio menjivar.com

## Tibia lamp, Studiomold

Tibia floor lamp by Studiomold is created using recycled materials.
www.studiomold.com

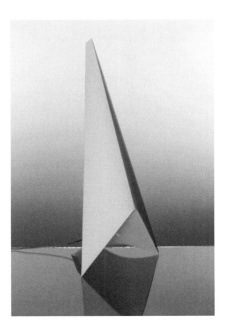

## Stealth flat-packed floor lamp, Blue Marmalade

Stealth is a flat-packed floor lamp designed specifically to be used with an energy-saving lightbulb. The shade is constructed entirely from long-wearing recyclable polypropylene, and can be easily dismantled for recycling after use.
www.bluemarmalade.co.uk

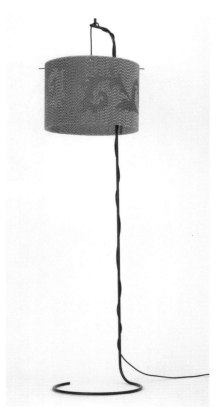

### Flute Standard lamp, Giles Miller, Farm Designs

Forming part of Giles Miller's Flute range, this standard lamp is produced from corrugated cardboard that is either recycled or sustainably sourced. The delicate floral pattern is hand-fluted into the surface of every piece of card creating a unique, hand-crafted, sustainable product.
www.farmdesigns.co.uk

### Bald lamp, Eugenio Menjivar

Eugenio Menjivar spent two years as a design consultant for the USAID and NGO program, Aid to Artisans, during which time he became aware that one of the main flaws with Salvadoran design production – the lack of raw materials – could be solved with one of the country's main problems: trash. Bald lamp is designed using scrap found around his native El Salvador.
wwweugenio menjivar.com

### Drunken Light, Andrew Oliver

Created from recycled, salvaged and secondhand furniture, Andrew Oliver's Drunken standard lamp zigzags to the floor.
www.andrewoliver designsandmakes. co.uk

## Big Crush lamp base, Brendan Young, Studiomold

Disused PET drinks bottles are crushed and painted black to form this sculptural lamp base. www.studiomold.co.uk

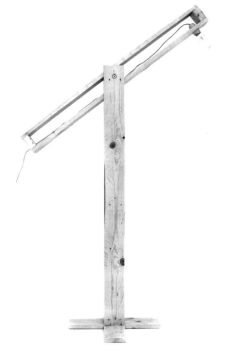

## Palette standard lamp, Nina Tolstrup

Rather than making and shipping the product itself, Nina Tolstrup sells the instructions on how to create her standard lamp yourself, from locally found pallets. www.studiomama. com

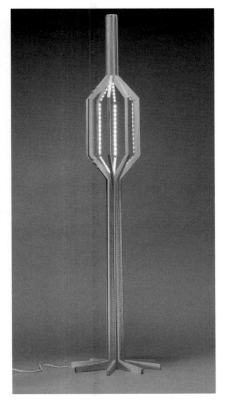

## Arbol floor lamp, Emiliano Godoy, Alejandro Castro and Alejandro Machorro, Godoylab, Pirwi

Assembled from eight identical pieces joined in a radial arrangement, Arbol imitates the trunks and branches of trees, where the strength of the whole comes from distributing the weight among the limbs. The lamp features modular LED boards and is manufactured in certified birch plywood, finished with non-toxic Livos varnish. www.pirwi.com

## Hey Chair floor lamp, Maarten Baas

Saving discarded furniture from landfill, Maarten Baas' assemblages give unwanted objects unexpected new functions, such as this floor lamps made up of old chairs. www.maartenbaas.com

## Non-Standard Lamp, Anna McConnell

Anna McConnell extends a product's life by adaptation rather than redesign. Her Non-Standard Lamp illustrates that rather than continuously replacing low-quality items you can adjust them to suit your needs. www.annamcconnell.co.uk

## Big Red Light, Regis R

Regis R transforms a motley assortment of discarded rubbish into his Big Red Light. r.egis.online.fr

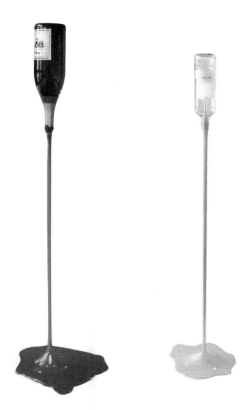

## Bottle Bulb Light,
## Steven Kessels and James
## Granger, Kessels Granger,
## Land Water & The Sky

Exploiting the colours and convenient shapes of reused glass bottles, the Bottle Bulb creates an ambient LED light while retaining the individual character of the original recycled material.
www.kesselgranger.com

## Floor lamps,
## Rachel Bending, Bird

Bird is a committed climate-neutral business (Australia's first) and also offset any carbon emissions created by their business. These floor lamps reflect their eco-friendly approach.
www.birdtextile.com.au

## Flame Lamp,
## Gitta Gschwendtner

Designed to showcase energy-efficient candle bulbs while alluding to the consumption of finite resources, Gitta Gschwendtner's Flame Lamps are a play on electric lights and are designed to create a sense of cosiness and tradition with their electric flame.
www.gittagschwendtner.com

## Aladdin floor lamp, Stuart Haygarth

Based on collections of different coloured glassware found in flea markets, car boot sales and junk shops, Stuart Haygarth's Aladdin groups together different shapes, textures and functions of glassware, united by their respective colours. The collections are housed in lightbox vitrines resembling museum showcases. www.stuarthaygarth.com

## Blocko lamp, Jim Church, Scrap Design

Glass bricks reclaimed from demolished factories are illuminated with long-lasting, low-energy LEDs to create an ambient light. www.scrapdesign.co.uk

## Tetra Lamp, Masif Designs

Tetra Lamps are inspired by the iconic Tetra Pak container. Each lamp is filled with an energy efficient LED and can be switched on or off simply by touching its base. www.masifdesigns.com

### Abyss free-standing floor lamp, Osko+Deichmann, Kundalini

Abyss is composed of a modular structure of recyclable polycarbonate illuminated by an LED strip. This vertebrate structure allows the lamp infinite combinations of self-standing articulated forms that appear to float freely in space.
www.kundalini.it

⚡ ♻

### Jar Jar Lights, Sebastian Hejna, Farm Designs

Sebastian Hejna transforms empty jars and bottles from familiar household brands into low-energy lights.
www.farmdesigns.co.uk

### Standard lamp, George Gold Furniture Design

Produced from sustainably sourced timbers and finished with natural, non-toxic oils, George Gold's beautifully crafted standard lamp is constructed to last a lifetime.
www.georgegoldfurnituredesign.co.uk

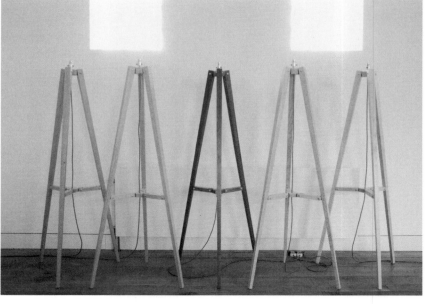

### Bolla light, Michael Sodeau, Gervasoni

Woven from fast growing and sustainable rattan, the Bolla light produces a warm, diffused glow. Designed to take a low-energy lightbulb, Bolla is also free from toxins.
www.gervasoni1882.it

### Silvana floor light, Max McMurdo, Reestore

By using a discarded or damaged washing machine drum, an energy-saving light bulb and recycled frosted glass, Reestore radically transform unwanted items into the Silvana floor light.
www.reestore.com

### Ticket Lamp, Elise Fouin

Built with a used roll of cashier paper and held in place with natural, non-toxic varnish, Elise Fouin's Ticket Lamp uses an energy-saving lightbulb to illustrate patterns of consumption.
www.elisefouin.com

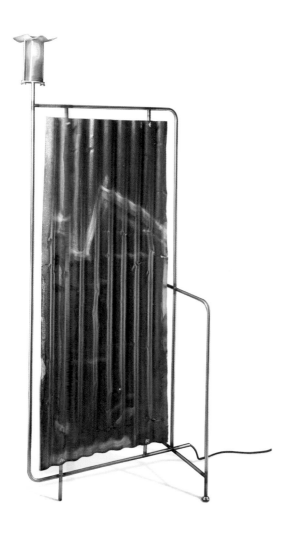

### Shanty floor light, Ryan Frank

Shanty is a floor-standing light that doubles as a room dividing screen. The screen is a simple sheet of old corrugated iron salvaged from East London and the whole piece can be easily dismantled for recycling.
www.ryanfrank.net

### Lucid standard lamp, Aki Kotkas

Oak, the leg of a bathtub, metal piping and stretched CDs combine to make Aki Kotkas' recycled lamp.
koti.welho.com/akotkas

### Frida desk lamp, Amy Adams, Perch!

Using low-impact materials and processes, all Perch! products are finished using non-toxic glazes – as is this quirky and colourful desk lamp.
www.perchdesign.net

### Vintage lamp, Design by Us

The base of Design by Us' Vintage lamp is constructed using a unique mix of recycled 1950s and 1960s glassware.
www.design-by-us.com

### Light to Drink, Alessandra Dallagiovanna, Davide Groppi

Light to Drink is an LED table lamp with interchangeable coloured diffusers.
www.davidegroppi.com

## Bottle-base lamp with bucket shade, Heath Nash

Heath Nash draws on his local South African craft tradition of using recycled plastic bottles and other objects to make new, desirable objects such as this lamp base and shade.
www.heathnash.com

## Apprentice Lamp, John D. O'Leary and Allan McIntyre, BlueGreen&Co

Made by trainees learning the traditional craft of wood turning, the Apprentice Lamp is built from an assortment of turned sections made from reclaimed wood. The complexity of each section is dependent on the experience and ability of the trainee, increasing in difficulty as their skills improve. With no two sections identical, an infinite variety of lamps are possible.
www.bluegreenandco.com

## Tiffany lamp, Regis R

Playing on the shape of the classic Tiffany lamp, Regis R transforms a motley assortment of discarded rubbish into this eco-friendly alternative.
r.egis.online.fr

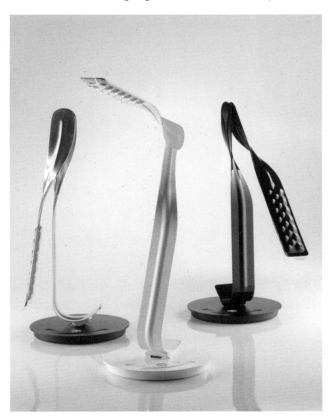

## Leaf task lamp, Yves Behar, Herman Miller

Leaf is an advanced LED task light that lasts 10 times longer and uses 40 percent less energy than compact fluorescent bulbs. The light is also made of 37 percent recycled materials, and is 95 percent recyclable at the end of its life.
www.fuseproject.com
www.hermanmiller.co.uk

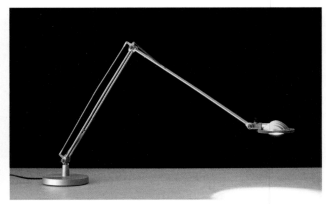

## Bend lamp, Michele Menescardi, Mr Smith Studio, Fontana Arte

Using 30 white LEDs, a sensory switch and a dimmer, Bend can be used as either a table, floor or wall lamp.
www.fontanaarte.it

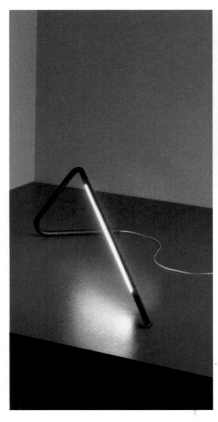

## Berenice task lamp, Alberto Meda, Paolo Rizzatto, Luceplan

Originally designed in 1985 by Paolo Rizzatto and Alberto Meda, Berenice is a recyclable aluminium task lamp, improved to make use of new, high-efficiency LED light sources.
www.luceplan.com

149

### No Tech lamp, Gregorio Spini, Kundalini

This stylish table lamp has a low-energy fluorescent spotlight made of an unbreakable, transparent and curved polycarbonate stem.
www.kundalini.it

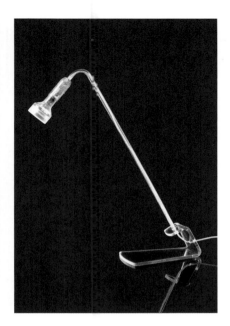

### Bill desk lamp, Tobias Grau

Tobias Grau's belief that good design should not only be beautiful and technically accomplished but also environmentally compatible applies not only to his products but also to his company's building, where 30 percent of the energy requirements are provided by photovoltaic systems. The Bill desk light is equally energy-efficient and is fitted with an 11W compact fluorescent lamp.
www.tobias-grau.com

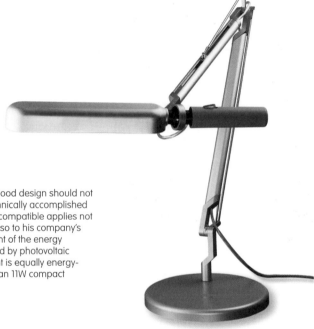

### Zed table lamp, Osvaldo Matos

Recycled from 100 percent post-consumer waste materials, the Zed light is an energy-efficient LED table lamp.
www.osvaldomatos.pt

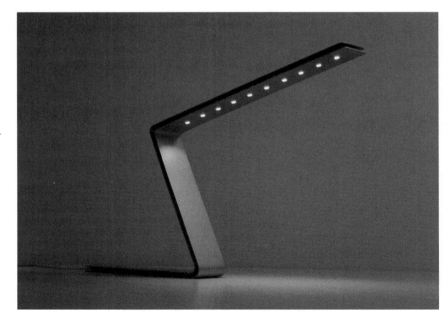

## Luau table lamp, Vessel

A bright tabletop light that is equally useful indoors and out, the Luau can be lit while charging, and lights up automatically when lifted from the base. It can also be dimmed or turned off in order to conserve energy until needed.
www.vessel.com

## Sun Jar, Tobias Young, Suck UK

Captured inside the Sun Jar is a highly efficient solar cell, rechargeable battery and low-energy LED lamps. When the jar is placed in sunlight the solar cell creates an electrical current that charges the battery over a few hours. This energy is then used at night to power the three LED lamps inside the jar.
www.suck.uk.com

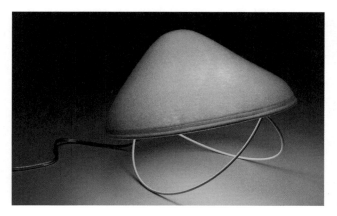

## Shroom lamp, Jaime Salm and Kate Wise, Mio

Made from 100 percent wool, the Shroom light is designed for easy disassembly to assist transportation and recycling. Using traditional felt moulding techniques and local manufacturers as a source of inspiration, the Shroom explores felt's natural suitability as a material for diffusing light.
www.mioculture.com

## Candeloo night light, Andreu Osika

A night light designed for children, Candeloo is safe, portable and rechargeable. The SafeCharge System eliminates exposed electrical contacts and they are always charged and ready to grab in the dark.
www.vesselinc.com

## Handl-EGGS with care, Mattia Frongia

Handl-EGGS with care is a handmade lamp, using real eggs covered in resin as a lightbulb. The eggs are illuminated with a low-energy LED and the original eggbox packaging is also used.
mattiafrongia@hotmail.it

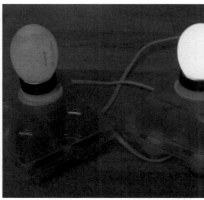

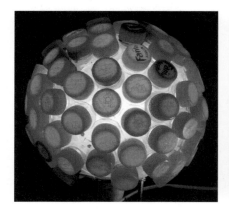

### CAPtivate,
### Lucy Norman,
### Lula Dot

Only 5.5 percent of plastic bottles sold in the UK are recycled, which leaves 40,000 tonnes going into landfill each year. Bottle caps are not generally recycled as they are made from a different plastic to the bottle. CAPtivate was designed to use this waste, turning it into an ambient light.
www.lucynorman.co.uk

### Luffa lampshade,
### Wyssem and Cecile Nochi

Wyssem and Cecile Nochi have transformed luffa gourds, which are typically used as bath sponges in the home, into natural, low-energy lampshades. The luffa seeds are intentionally left in the plant to allow the user to replant them.
www.wyssemnochi.com

## Packaging Lamp,
## David Gardener

David Gardener's paper pulp lamp is made entirely from the packaging used to transport its electronic components. The lamp also takes an energy-saving bulb.
www.davidgardener.co.uk

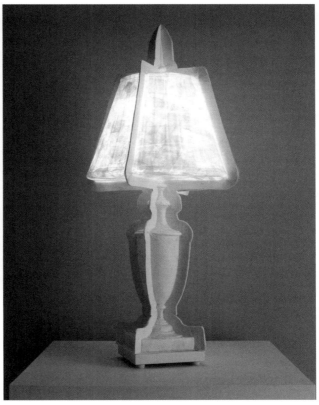

### Harry Allen lamp, Areaware

Forming part of the 'Reality' series, which consists of objects whose form is 'sampled' from existing sources, Harry Allen's Lamp is simply formed from ricepaper and glue.
www.areaware.com

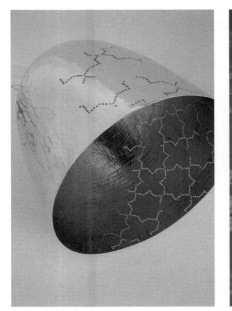

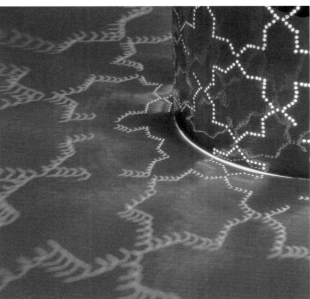

### Listrik lamp, We Made

A fairtrade collaboration between Dutch designers and Indonesian craftspeople, the Listrik light uses recycled aluminium to create an ambient light.
www.lidewij.net
www.rixxt.nl

### Nod lamp, Andrew Lang

Winner of an Energy Saving Trust Award, Nod is a wall-mounted bedside light with a central recess to store a book. Mobile phones and MP3 players can be stored and charged in the adjacent holes while you sleep. The lamp source is an energy-efficient T5 lamp with electronic ballast.
www.andrewlang.co.uk

### Saturnus lamp, Antoinet Deurloo and Michael Bom, Atelier Bom Design

Saturnus is constructed from recycled vinyl records and uses an energy-saving lightbulb.
www.bomdesign.nl

### Eco Desk 36, Luminair

With a hand-turned sustainable walnut frame and shade, the Eco Desk 36 is an ecologically made desk lamp with a 36 LED cool or warm cluster light head. The light is also touch sensitive and features a dimming control point within the shade.
www.nigelsecostore.com

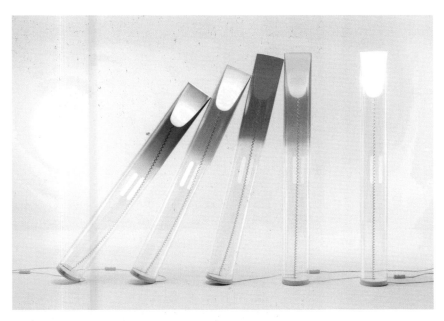

## Toobe lamp, Ferrucio Lavini, Kartell

Toobe comes equipped with a fluorescent energy-saving lightbulb, an eco-compatible alternative to the classic incandescent bulb. This lasts up to 10 times longer and consumes up to 5 times less energy than an ordinary bulb. www.kartell.it

## Lab Lamp, Krejci

Made from old computer circuit boards, Krejci's Lab Lamp saves toxic chemicals from becoming harmful landfill. www.krejci.nl

### Lastra lamp,
### Rona M. Koblenz,
### RMK Design

Lastra is a sustainable table light made using high-flux LED technology integrated in to a specially designed printed circuit board that enables the white LED to perform at its highest standards.
www.rmkdesign.co.uk

### Beryl and Friends lamps,
### WEmake

WEmake rescue lamps and shades that have fallen out of favour, and rewire and refit them with low-energy bulbs before lovingly preserving them in a shrink-wrapped jacket. This process magically reinterprets the original aesthetic while leaving the original light fully functional to be revived at some future date.
www.wemake.co.uk

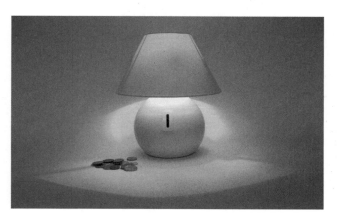

### Prepay Lamp,
### Jethro Macey

Turned on for a fixed amount of time by a coin-operated switch, Prepay Lamp heightens awareness of electricity consumption while encouraging you to save your cash.
www.jethromacey.com

## Chrysanth lampshade, Nicola Prodromou, Use UK

Use UK was set up with the aim of making eco-friendly products and encouraging environmental awareness in interior design. Their lampshades are made from 100 percent recycled cardboard (80 percent post-consumer waste and 20 percent post-manufacture waste) and are printed with limited-edition patterns such as the Chrysanth design. www.use-uk.com

## Transport lamp, Tomoko Azumi, Twentytwentyone

Constructed from sustainably sourced timber, Tomoko Azumi's Transport Lamp is a portable lamp in beech wood with a Tyvek shade. It is simply constructed from a flat-pack kit, which reduces the product's carbon footprint, as every cubic cm is crucial for fuel saving during goods transportation. www.twentytwentyone.com

# Kitchens & Bathrooms

### Everhot 100 Electric Range, Everhot

As well as having an energy saving design and low electricity requirements, Everhot electric ranges feature an ECO control to provide continual heat output at a low rate of energy consumption. The Everhot factory is also powered using sustainable energy sourced from a 13th Century water mill.
www.everhot.co.uk

### Heat Storage Cooker, Aga

Since the first model was introduced more than 80 years ago, 70 percent of each cooker has been made from previously used material such as gearboxes, guttering, drain covers and lampposts. Furthermore, models that have reached the end of their long lives are recycled into new ones, thus completing the loop. Aga have also recently developed biofuel-ready cookers.
www.aga-rayburn.co.uk

### Cold Block/Vegetable Box, David Weatherhead

Intending to promote a downsizing of refrigerators, David Weatherhead uses the natural cooling properties of terracotta and water to cold-store vegetables and fruit without the use of electricity. His designs are available as a fitted cabinet, or a vegetable box with a chopping board lid made from sustainable beech.
www.davidweatherhead.com

## Cinque Terre Kitchen, Schiffini

Offering fully recyclable kitchens built from non-polluting materials, Schiffini use only sustainably sourced wood and produce panels made of 100 percent recycled materials. All paints and glues used are free from toxins and the cabinets are dry-assembled, without adhesive.
www.schiffini.com

## Spezie Kitchen, Schiffini

Fully recyclable kitchens made from sustainably sourced wood and aluminium, Schiffini kitchens are also characterized by their use of toxin-free materials and a commitment to reducing harmful emissions.
www.schiffini.com

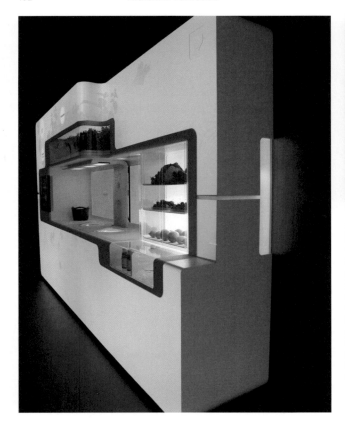

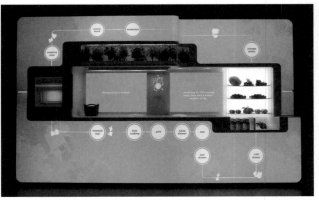

## Green Kitchen, Whirlpool

Set within a framed wall-unit, Green kitchen is a development project by Whirlpool that utilizes their latest energy-saving appliances and demonstrates how they can be used together to optimize the use of heat and water, reducing energy bills by up to 70 percent. The system diverts up to 60 percent of the water and heat generated from appliances to fuel other appliances, allowing huge amounts of energy to be saved or reused.
www.whirlpool.co.uk

## Kitchen, Milestone

Producing the UK's first kitchens made solely from recycled materials and those from well managed resources, Milestone has a very strong environmental policy that runs all the way through the company, from using only FSC approved timber to converting waste paper into bedding for animals.
www.milestone.uk.net

## Pay it Back
## kitchen island,
## Alexandra
## Sten Jørgensen

A model of how nature and consumption are connected, the Pay it Back kitchen island is a sink, table and composting area. As the green box fills up, the compost is used along with waste water from the sink to feed a climbing plant on the side of the unit. The life of the plant is dependent on how well you adapt to ethical living.
annealexandra@gmail.com

## Kitchen
## and worktop,
## Durat

Durat is a solid polyester-based material used for custom made surfaces in public and private interiors. Ideal for kitchens and worksurfaces, the material contains recycled plastics and is itself 100 percent recyclable.
www.durat.com

### Flat XL storage unit, Benedini Association, Agape

This storage unit is made from Parapan®, an ecological material made without solvents. Parapan® is a solid and uniformly coloured material that can be completely recycled and, thanks to its acrylic base, it is completely waterproof and is particularly suited to use in the bathroom.
www.agapedesign.it

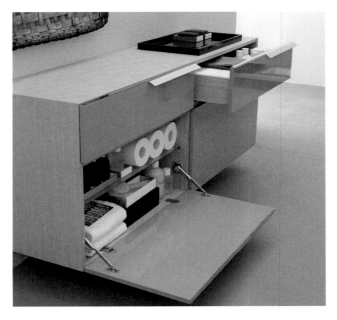

### Yume combined washbasin/washstand, Matteo Nunziati, Rapsel

Moulded out of Nikron® a 100 percent recyclable, silky-smooth, high-tech material, Yume was created for a major project fair in Dubai and draws inspiration from twentieth-century abstract minimalism.
www.rapsel.it

### Infinity modular unit, Nespoli and Novara, Rapsel

Infinity is an adaptable, modular bathroom system comprising units and basins made from 100 percent recyclable Parapan®. The units can be placed in a gridded, symmetrical formation or offset to create a Mondrian-like effect.
www.rapsel.it

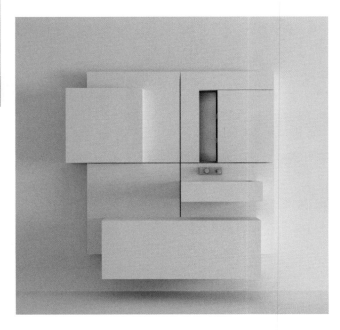

### Shower curtain, Transylvanian Images

Made from recycled vintage fabric woven on handlooms in narrow widths and then sewn together so that the raw, slightly rougher edges show, Transylvanian Images' linen and cotton blend shower curtain provides a welcome respite from the standard plastic versions.
www.transylvanian images.com

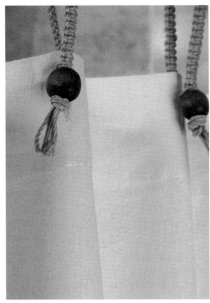

### Hemp shower curtain, Draper's Organic

Made of hemp fibre, Draper's Organic's shower curtain makes the most of this eco-friendly material. Hemp can be grown without pesticides, replenishes soil with nutrients, controls erosion of the topsoil, and produces a large amount of oxygen.
www.drapersorganic cotton.co.uk

### Shower restrictor and dual flush WC, Ideal Standard

Showers can use anything from 10 to over 30 litres (2½ to 8 gallons) of water per minute depending on the water pressure. A shower restrictor limits the water flow to 9 litres (2⅓ gallons) per minute at 3 bar. A dual flush cistern can also save 33 percent of water when you use the small flush button.
www.idealstandard.com

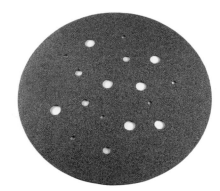

### Digital shower, Touchtile

Touchtile is a digital shower system that provides instant water control. The shower has five preset flow-rates including a low or eco flow setting.
www.touchtile.com

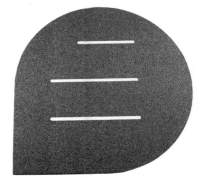

### Bath mats, Simple Forms

Using sustainable cork from their native Portugal, Simple Forms' bathmats are helping to revive traditional production methods, which have recently been falling into decline. The results are practical, simple and eco-friendly.
www.simpleformsdesign.com

## Factor Sink, Marike

Factor is a minimalist sink that embodies Marike's increased commitment to recycling of raw materials. Its gently sloping surface is cast in a recycled material of 94 percent quartz and 6 percent resin.
www.marike.net

## Washbasin, Benedini Association, Agape

Rectangular crystal-glass inset washbasin without overflow, with removable sloping surface made from environmentally friendly, 100 percent recyclable Parapan®.
www.agapedesign.it

## Alto Click technology tap, Ideal Standard

Resistance is felt in the lever of the Alto tap when the tap is delivering half of the potential water flow. When the lever 'clicks', the water flow is increased to normal. If the lever is stopped before the click then water usage is cut by 50 percent.
www.idealstandard.com

## Sink, Simple Forms

Simple Forms use locally sourced, sustainable cork in innovative and unexpected ways. Designs such as their sink combine many of the qualities of this underused and unique wood.
www.simpleformsdesign.com

## Oval bath, Ulla Koskinen, Ulla Tuominen and Eeva Lithovius, Durat

Made from recycled plastics, a Durat bath is extremely durable and 100 percent recyclable. Durat is easy to keep clean, resistant to various chemicals and can be renewed with light sanding if necessary.
www.durat.com

## Square taps, Benedini Association, Agape

These polished or satin-finished stainless steel taps have a floor-mounted gradual control single-lever mixer tap and an electronic sensor to regulate and reduce water consumption.
www.agapedesign.it

## Bathroom, Ulla Koskinen, Ulla Tuominen and Eeva Lithovius, Durat

Durat is a solid polyester-based material containing recycled plastics. It is extremely durable and 100 percent recyclable. This bathroom, constructed from Durat, is easy to keep clean and resistant to various chemicals. The surface can be renewed with light sanding if required.
www.durat.com

## Shower tray, Ulla Koskinen, Ulla Tuominen and Eeva Lithovius, Durat

Made from recycled plastics, a Durat shower tray is durable and 100 percent recyclable. Durat is easy to keep clean, resistant to various chemicals and can always be renewed with light sanding if necessary.
www.durat.com

## Alto water saving bath, Ideal Standard

With a reduced capacity of 149 litres (39 gallons), the bath saves approximately 15 percent of water.
www.idealstandard.com

## Motion tap, Hansa

Hansa's Motion is fitted with a Hansa Eco Control cartridge, providing an adjustable water quantity limit and reducing water usage by up to 50 percent. It can be activated whenever required and set to the desired flow rate.
www.hansataps.com

## Arya tap, Bandini

The Arya is made in VetroFreddo®, a 100 percent recyclable resin. It has an unconventional design, producing a wide sweep of water but at a lower flow rate than ordinary hand washing taps.
www.rbandini.it

## Axor range, Philippe Starck, Hansgrohe

Axor is a friendly-looking product range from Hansgrohe, produced in accordance with their strong environmental policy. The German production plant uses solar panels to produce energy and more than 90 percent of waste is recycled. Even the packaging material is recycled wherever possible, and no plastics or bubblewrap are used.
www.hansgrohe.co.uk

### Cera toilet, IFO

A low water consumption toilet, Ifo's Cera provides reliable one-flush operation.
www.ifosanitar.com

### Foam-Flush Toilet, Clivus Multrum

Using a mix of alcohol-based soap, water and air, the Foam-Flush Toilet creates a foam blanket that moves waste to a composter, reducing the amount of water used for flushing by over 97 percent. The soap is completely compatible with the composting process, and the foam helps to keep the toilet bowl clean.
www.clivusmultrum.com

### Flushwise toilet, Twyford

Using just 2.6 litres (³/₄ gallon) for the short flush and 4 litres (1 gallon) for the full one, the Flushwise saves 6 litres (1 ¹/₂ gallons) of water per flush compared to an average toilet. This adds up to an annual saving of 30,000 litres (7,925 gallons) every year in an average family home.
www.twyfordbathrooms.com

# Textiles

### Reprinted waste fabric, Caroline Till

Caroline Till's work focuses on the issue of waste, in particular the staggering volume of textile material that is discarded to landfill sites each year. An estimated one million tons of textiles is thrown away each year in the UK, and she reprints as much as she can in her unique painterly and graphic style.
caroline@carolinetill.com

### Vilske fabric, Fokus Fabrik

Fokus Fabric's designs are printed on a mix of organic cotton and hemp. Hemp is naturally resistant to pests and weeds, eliminating the need for pesticides.
www.fokusfabrik.fi

### Lucia fabric, Camira

Produced from 100 percent post-industrial waste diverted away from landfill, this fabric uses environmentally friendly, non-metallic dyestuffs and is based on a cradle-to-cradle concept.
www.camirafabrics.com

### Koneisto fabric, Fokus Fabrik

Inspired by the contrast of nature in a pulsing urban landscape, Finnish designers Fokus Fabrik choose to design and produce their collection in Finland, ensuring ethical production.
www.fokusfabrik.fi

## Reused bed linen, Muji

Muji rescues leftover yarn from fabric production to create their Reused products, which are not re-dyed and so are randomly patterned.
www.mujionline.co.uk

## 2 Row Satin Stitch bed linen, Luma

All Luma bed linen is made under fairtrade conditions using organic cotton certified by the Dutch agency, Control Union which is recognized by the Soil Association. This means that every stage of production has been independently inspected to ensure that neither the environment nor anyone's health has been damaged during the process.
www.lumadirect.com

## Crochetta bed linen, Luma

Bedding made using luxurious 'long-staple' organic cotton. Luma is dedicated to creating beautiful home textiles, made from luxurious organic cottons and environmentally-friendly linens and silks.
www.lumadirect.com

## Meadow Flowers duvet cover, Aravali, Traidcraft

Block printed using vegetable dyes on 100 percent cotton, the Meadow Flowers duvet cover is made in India by Aravali. The fairtrade company was set up in 1976 and promotes many of the traditional products made by craftspeople who live and work in the culturally rich state of Rajasthan.
www.traidcraft.co.uk

### Cove bed linen, Amenity Home

Each limited-edition print featured on Amenity Home's Cove bed linen is printed using non-toxic, water-based, eco-friendly dyes onto organic, SKAL certified, 300 thread-count cotton percale. The design is printed domestically and sewn locally.
www.amenityhome.com

### Mocha bed linen, Traidcraft

This 100 percent organic cotton bed linen in mocha has a 200 thread-count, making it strong and super-soft.
www.traidcraft.co.uk

### Hand-quilted bedspread, Luma

Hand-quilted in pure silk and filled with Kapok fibre, each Luma bedspread is crafted in a fairtrade environment.
www.lumadirect.com

### Tie duvet cover, Liv UK

Woven from exceptionally soft and durable 220 thread-count 100 percent organic and fairtrade cotton percale, this classic bed linen uses ties for fastenings on the duvets and pillowcases.
www.liv-uk.com

### Organic bed linen, The White Company

Organic cotton grown without pesticides or chemical fertilizer is used to produce The White Company's organic bed linen range. The entire production process, including the weaving process and the dyes and chemicals used is inspected and certified by Skal International, a subsidiary of the Control Union World Group, to ensure that the product does not harm the environment.
www.thewhite company.com

### Tie pillowcase, Liv UK

Like the matching duvet cover, this pillowcase is woven from 220 thread-count 100 percent organic fairtrade cotton percale.
www.liv-uk.com

## Blankets and throws, Luma

Made by rural cooperatives and recognized fairtrade producers, Luma's beautiful blankets and throws come with a label recording the name and village of the maker.
www.lumadirect.com

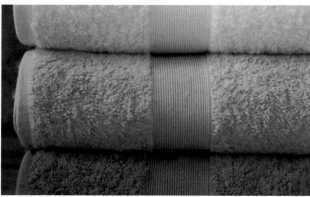

## Albatross hand towels, The Lazy Environmentalist

Manufactured in Peru from Control Union certified organic cotton, Albatross towels are exceptionally deep, absorbent and cosy. The cotton, obtained from small farmers on fairtrade principles, is dyed using low-impact limestone and flax.
www.lazyenvironmentalist.com

## Natural Hyacinth cushion, Biome Lifestyle

Hand woven from the water hyacinth plant and cut to reveal the inside of the stem, this sustainable product has a truly unique, rough, bark-like appearance. The back of the cushion is covered in natural hessian, while the natural stems of the hyacinth can be used to massage the base of the back.
www.biomelifestyle.com

### Hemp bedlinen, Jilly Cholmondeley

More environmentally friendly than cotton, Jilly Cholmondeley's luxurious hemp bedlinen is sourced and woven in Italy. Hemp has natural antibacterial qualities, it improves with age and it lasts for years.
www.jillycholmondeley.com

### Organic cotton bath sheet, Biome Lifestyle

This organic cotton fairtrade bath sheet has not received the highly caustic industrial wash usually given to cotton towels. As a result it requires a few normal domestic washes to bring out its true softness and absorbency. The cotton used is grown organically to reduce pesticide use, and is imported on fairtrade terms.
www.biomelifestyle.com

### Luxor towels, The White Company

The White Company's super-absorbent luxury towels are made from 600 g (1 ⅓ lb) pure organic cotton.
www.thewhitecompany.com

## Organic cotton towels, The White Company

Available in white or ecru, only eco-friendly dyes and chemicals are used to produce the purest white, without the need for bleach.
www.thewhitecompany.com

## Mocha flannel, Liv UK

Liv UK's 100 percent organic and fairtrade 550 g (1 1/4 lb) cotton terry towelling face cloth is soft, super-absorbent and sourced from India.
www.liv-uk.com

## Organic towels, Habitat

Produced from organic cotton, Habitat's range of organic towels are available in various sizes.
www.habitat.co.uk

## Towels, Liv UK

Liv UK's luxurious bath sheets produced from soft, 100 percent organic cotton, are produced under fairtrade conditions in India.
www.liv-uk.com

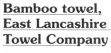

## Bamboo towel, East Lancashire Towel Company

Bamboo thrives without the use of pesticides and is a natural cellulose fibre that can be converted into yarn without the addition of chemicals. These bamboo towels are woven using bamboo for the pile and cotton for the backing, giving a moisture absorption rate three times that of standard cotton. Bamboo fibre is also antibacterial, antifungal, anti-static and is 100 percent biodegradable.
www.towelcompany.co.uk

## Towels, Luma

Luma's organic cotton towels have a wonderful deep pile, are thick, soft, and super-absorbent. Finished with a subtle ribbed border, the towels are dyed with environmentally friendly dyes and made in India under fairtrade conditions.
www.lumadirect.com

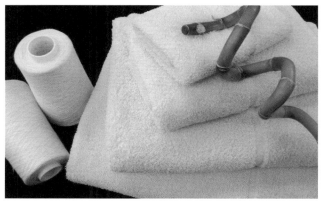

## Plain fabric rolls, Transylvanian Images

Using the finest vintage, hand-processed, handspun, organic hemp and boiled linen, woven on authentic handlooms, Transylvanian Images aim to educate consumers by establishing a market for these wonderful products. The company strives to create jobs for villagers in Transylvania and to encourage the use of natural fibres. They sell fabric both by the metre and as completed items.
www.transylvanianimages.com

## Reclaimed wool throw, Biome Lifestyle

Woven from 100 percent reclaimed unwanted mill-waste yarn, this wool throw is made by a small family company in Scotland.
www.biomelifestyle.com

## Sonic woven textile, Alyce Santoro, Designtex

An audible, multi-purpose textile woven from reclaimed cassette tape, Sonic is designed by artist Alyce Santoro as part of her focus on new uses for post-industrial waste. As a 100 percent polyester product, Sonic is extremely durable, its strength derived from the thickness of the tape. Sounds in the weave can actually be heard by drawing a tape head from a reconfigured Sony Walkman over its surface.
www.designtex.com

## Organic printed wovens, Caroline Till

As well as huge environmental problems, the globalization of the textile industry has fractured manufacturing supply routes, allowing many exploitative working conditions to occur. Caroline Till addresses these problems with her organic, fairtrade fabric range for interiors. The range fuses hi- and low-technology with painterly and graphic styles.
caroline@carolinetill.com

## Oxygen fabric, Camira

Oxygen is a 100 percent climate-neutral fabric. The amount of carbon dioxide produced during manufacture has been carefully analyzed and verified by Climate Care and the price of every metre includes an amount, which the company invest in carbon-offsetting projects.
www.camirafabrics.com

## Spiral mat, Celia Suzanne Sluijter

Celia Suzanne Sluijter's aim is to alleviate poverty and improve production methods in the area where her products are made; in this case Nepal and Tibet.
www.xoplus.nl

## Pure undyed cashmere cushion, Biome Lifestyle

Made from the purest Scottish cashmere and finished with natural shell buttons, this hand-spun cushion is undyed and chemical free.
www.biomelifestyle.com

## Forget-Me-Not cushions, Barley Massey

Providing comfort on a physical and emotional level, Forget-Me-Not items are designed to help the user to heal following the loss of a loved one. The cushions and blankets are made from reused clothing provided by the customer and addresses the difficult subject of death in a positive and creative manner.
www.fabrications1.co.uk

## Hungarian sack cushion, Biome Lifestyle

Handmade in London using reused Hungarian grain sacks dating from 1910 to 1930, these cushions are hand woven with flax linen, known for its durability and strength. The varying stripes and initials on the cushions indicate the weaver and the particular mill they came from.
www.biomelifestyle.com

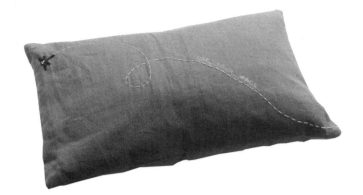

### Use Your Wings cushion, Bridget West, Pieces of You

Made from an old blue shirt and khaki trousers, this cushion gives a new life to unwanted items of clothing.
www.piecesofyou.co.uk

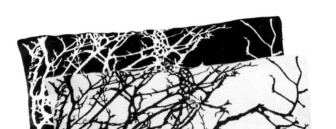

### Branches Paperpillow, Celia Suzanne Sluijter

Derived from a Himalayan plant that can be processed into paper, Celia Suzanne Sluijter's Paperpillows are surprisingly strong and washable.
www.xoplus.nl

### Cushions, Casa Copenhagen

Casa Copenhagen's range of cushions is produced from organic cotton.
www.casacopenhagen.com

### Cushions, Nicola Prodromou, Use UK

Use UK was set up with the aim of making eco-friendly products more desirable to the design-conscious. Nicola Prodromou uses fabric rescued from textile sample books that would otherwise have gone into landfill. The samples are sourced from high-quality manufacturers, yet are now considered out of date.
www.use-uk.com

## Tapestry cushions, Frédérique Morrel

Based on the reworking of vintage needlework, Frédérique Morrel's cushions give old tapestries a new lease of life.
www.frederique morrel.com

## Blue stripe cushion covers, Transylvanian Images

Transylvanian images recycle vintage grain sacks into cushion covers. The pieces are made in a fairtrade environment in Transylvanian villages.
www.transylvanian images.com

## Cushions, Bird

Recognized as Australia's first climate neutral business in 2004, Bird products are made using solar power and low-impact local production methods. Bird also offset any carbon emissions created by their business. In addition, the hand-drawn botanical designs on their cushions are all hand printed using water-based dyes on natural, organic fabrics.
www.birdtextile.com.au

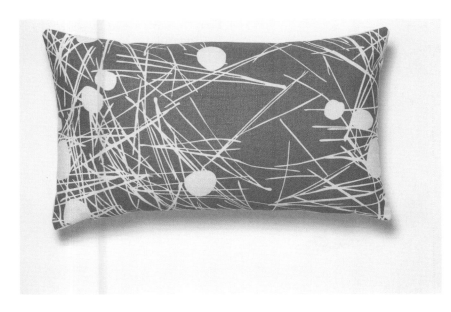

## Trail cushion, Amenity Home

Amenity Home offer a selection of two sustainable cushion inserts: one filled with high-quality fibres generated from recycled plastic bottles and the other filled with kapok.
www.amenityhome.com

## Colour Cushion, Thomas Eyck, Scholten & Baijings

Made from sustainable wool and cotton, this super-soft Colour Cushion makes use of lengths of coloured yarn.
www.scholtenbaijings.com

## Alpaca cushions, Josh Riley and Jaqueline Vitali, Moluche

Individually hand-woven in Chile and Peru from hand-spun organic alpaca, these cushions are modern, functional designs that remain true to the ideals and techniques used in the traditional work of the artisans who create them.
www.moluche.com

### Handle with Care cushions, Bridget West, Pieces of You

Handle with Care is made using recycled textiles and their care labels so that each cushion is completely unique.
www.piecesofyou.co.uk

### No Logo cushion, Bridget West, Pieces of You

Made from recycled textiles and their labels, each No Logo design is totally individual.
www.piecesofyou.co.uk

### Delicates cushion, Bridget West, Pieces of You

Bridget West's quirky Delicates design, digitally printed onto organic hemp cotton canvas, plays on the idea of textile care labels, alluding to the way in which our environment must be handled with care.
www.piecesofyou.co.uk

### Pompom cushion, Allpa, Traidcraft

Decorated with colourful pompoms, this bold, hand-woven striped cushion is produced in Peru by Allpa, a fairtrade company that markets crafts for producers in various parts of Peru. Any producers working with Allpa can access loans so they can afford to buy raw materials in advance of craft production.
www.traidcraft.co.uk

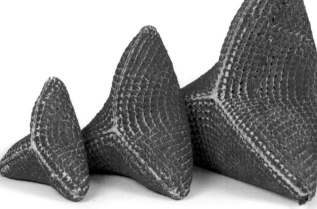

### Fatay cushions, Tramando

Recycled materials from the textile industry are crocheted to form Brazillian design group Tramando's tactile Fatay cushions.
www.tramando.com

### River cushion, Amenity Home

Using colours and designs taken from nature, Amenity Home's sustainable cushions are made from organic cotton blended with hemp.
www.amenityhome.com

## Recycled tube and bus seat-fabric cushions, Creatively Recycled Empire

Working towards producing a zero-waste future and proving the business case for sustainability, Creative Recycled Empire provided the London tube and bus network with special bins in which to place used upholstered seating. The unwanted fabric is then transformed into hardwearing cushions.
www.creativelyrecycledempire.co.uk

## Reclaimed seatbelt cushion, Biome Lifestyle

Made from recycled seatbelts, these innovative cushions are produced without unsightly seams or zips.
www.biomelifestyle.com

## River Paperpillows, Celia Suzanne Sluijter

The paper-making process used in making a Paperpillow is supported by Nepalokta, a fairtrade organization.
www.xoplus.nl

## Seville cushion, Michelle Mason, Eco Age

Michelle Mason's trademark abstract floral silhouettes emblazon her unbleached cotton Seville cushion.
www.eco-age.com

## Flutterby lumbar cushion, Selina Rose, Eco Age

Made from 100 percent wool felt and coloured using environmentally friendly dyes, the Flutterby lumbar cushion features heat-transferred decals of fluttering butterflies. www.eco-age.com

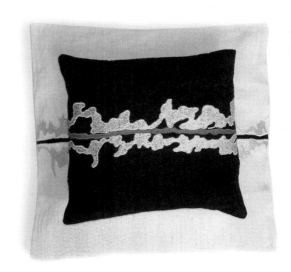

## River Paper Cushions, Celia Suzanne Sluijter

These hand embroidered cushions are made under fairtrade conditions in Nepal and form part of Celia Suzanne Sluijter's XO+ collection. www.xoplus.nl

## Nagarkot cushions, Celia Suzanne Sluijter

The Nagarkot cushions are made by women in Nepal and form part of Celia Suzanne Sluijter's XO+ collection. www.xoplus.nl

## Flutterby three-dimensional cushion, Selina Rose, Eco Age

Felt made from 100 percent wool and coloured using environmentally friendly dyes is water cut to produce the decorative three-dimensional effect on Selina Rose's Flutterby cushion. www.eco-age.com

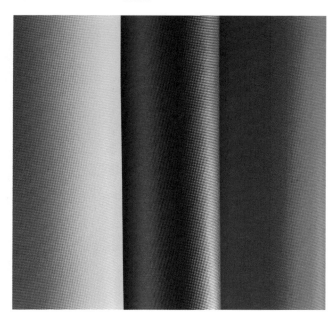

### Waterborn 2 fabric, Kvadrat

Constructed from sustainable fibres, this fabric has been awarded the EU Flower certificate for environmentally-friendly products.
www.kvadrat.dk

### Climatex Lifecycle fabric, Designtex

Designtex was the first company to create a closed-loop, cradle-to-cradle design for textiles. Climatex Lifecycle is a compostable biological nutrient that is designed to turn back into soil at the end of its life. Every dye chemical has been proven non-toxic. The water flowing out of the plant at the end of the manufacturing process is safe to drink, and all waste trimmings are felted and then sold to farmers as mulch.
www.designtex.com

### Hallingdal Fabric, Kvadrat

Awarded the EU Flower certificate, Kvadrat's Hallingdal fabric is guaranteed to be environmentally friendly.
www.kvadrat.dk

### Molly fabric, Åsa Pärson, Kvadrat

Molly by Kvadrat has been awarded the EU Flower certificate. This ensures the production process of the fabric has been proven to be environmentally friendly.
www.kvadrat.dk

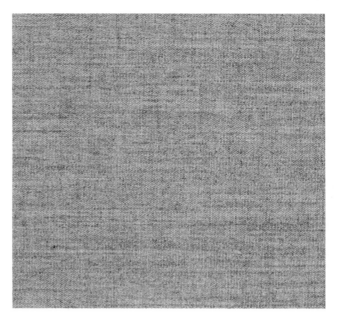

### Hemp fabric, Draper's Organic

Draper's Organic supply natural organic hemp by the metre. The sustainable and environmentally friendly fabric is available in a variety of naturally dyed colours and finishes.
www.drapersorganic
cotton.co.uk

### Fabrics, Muchatela, Design Connection Argentine Group

Using natural plant dyes from the 'Cordoba Sierras', Brazilian designer Muchatela creates a palette so bright and vivid it could easily be confused with synthetic dyes.
www.muchatela.
com.ar

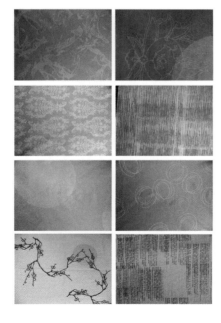

### Ultimate Floppy Linen, Emily Todhunter, O Eco Textiles

Grown in northern Italy without the use of herbicides, pesticides or synthetic fertilizers, Ultimate Floppy Linen is certified organic. The linen fibres used in the yarn are extremely long and have been spun and dyed by an Italian spinner who has earned the 'Master of Linen' designation. These craftspeople use only low-impact fibre-reactive dyes with no toxins. They also take care to treat their wastewater to avoid contamination.
www.oecotextiles.com

## Lavender Birdies, Claire Nicolson, All Things Original

Claire Nicolson's Birdies are made using vintage fabrics and filled with lavender.
www.allthingsoriginal.com

## Recycled Knit hot water bottle cover, Asaplab

Placing an emphasis on ethical and sustainable consumption, Italian design company Asaplab have designed a hot water bottle cover as part of their Recycled Knit collection. The project takes disused knitted garments and transforms them into new items of clothing and homeware.
www.asaplab.it

## Draught excluder, Bird

Designed to insulate your home and save energy, this draught excluder is hand printed using water-based dyes on organic fabric.
www.birdtextile.com.au

## Funky Chicken doorstop, Refab

Made from vintage and reclaimed fabrics, Refab's Funky Chicken doorstop is transported flat-packed, ready to be filled with rice at home. The company's aim is to keep packaging as environmentally friendly as possible so filling instructions are printed on recycled card and the product is wrapped in a biodegradable cellophane wrapper from sustainable forest sources.
www.refab.co.uk

### Eternal Lace fabric, Laura Marsden

Handmade using waste plastic bags rather than traditional yarns, Laura Marsden's Eternal Lace is supple, hardwearing and flexible, giving it huge potential for application.
www.lauramarsden.com

### Mobile, Roberta Cosulich

Produced locally at a fairtrade workshop in São Paulo, Brazil, Roberta Cosulich's mobile contains a fibre derived from the banana tree, highlighting the possibilities of this natural Brazilian material.
r.cosulich@iedbrasil.com.br

### Die-cut Ingeo™ fabric, Designtex

Derived from cornstarch, this lightweight, 100 percent Ingeo™ fabric has a three-dimensional quality created by fusing, embossing and die-cutting with a swirling, circular cut-out pattern. The natural origins of the fabric allow it to biodegrade at the end of its useful life – making it a closed-loop, sustainable product.
www.designtex.com

# Decorative Accessories

## Hay Vase, Anne Black

Available in different sizes, Anne Black's Hay Vases are handcrafted in a fairtrade workshop in Vietnam, and finished with a non-toxic glaze.
www.anneblack.dk

## Flopy Chiquita crocheted vase, Tramando, Design Connection Argentine Group

Woven with recycled waste material from the textile industry, Flopy Chiquita is a handmade crocheted vase, mounted on a ceramic base.
www.tramando.com

## tranSglass glassware collection, Tord Boontje and Emma Woffenden, Artecnica

An exquisite glassware collection handcrafted from recycled bottles, tranSglass embodies a design-conscious, environmentally aware aesthetic. With the help of Aid to Artisans, a non-profit organization that provides assistance to artisans worldwide, each vessel is handmade by skilled artisans in Guatemala, who expertly reinvent the glass bottles one at a time.
www.artecnicainc.com

### Animal Vase, Studiomold

The Animal Vase comprises a reused sherry glass with a choice of toy creature imprisoned for eternity inside a heat-shrunk skin. Each vase is unique, as they are all individually handmade with random disused and unwanted toy animals. Expect to see anything from dinosaurs or lions to horses and bisons stretching through the skin.
www.studiomold.co.uk

### Archetype Big vase, Carola Zee

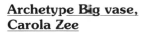

This design originated from an old mould that was thrown away by a mould maker when the model went out of fashion. By reusing the form, enlarging it and adding a new floral design to it, this cast-off mould has regained a new life.
www.carolazee.nl

### Campy Planters, Perch!

Made of earthenware and finished in a non-toxic glaze, Campy Planters are ideal for succulents, cacti or other small plants.
www.perchdesign.net

### Jupe vase, Biome Lifestyle

Handmade in naturally dried stoneware, the Jupe vase is fashioned from sustainable materials and shipped by sea to avoid unnecessary air miles.
www.biomelifestyle.com

### Bud Vases, Esque Studio

Esque Studio's Bud Vases are made from recycled beer bottles, which are melted and distorted in an ultra-efficient, wind-powered furnace until they are almost unrecognizable.
www.esque-studio.com

### Constructor vases, Lidewij Spitshuis and Rixt Reitsma, We Made

We Made is the result of a collaboration between Dutch designers Rixt Reitsma and Lidewij Spitshuis, with the Indonesian fairtrade organization Apikri. The Constructor ceramic vases are inspired by a fusion of Dutch architecture and the local crafts on the isle of Java.
www.lidewij.net
www.rixxt.nl

## Tina vessel, Sarah Thirlwell

Using homegrown timber, coloured acrylics and recycled plastics, Sarah produces a range of vessels that challenge contemporary craft techniques. The Tina vessel is crafted from FSC certified birch plywood and vending-cup plastic.
www.sarahthirlwell.com

## Recycled glass vase, Stephen Burks, Cappellini

Made of recycled glass mosaic, Cappellini's vase forms part of 'Cappellini Love', a sustainable-design project that promotes fairtrade and quality craftsmanship in fragile economies.
www.cappellini.it

## Bamboo Bulb vase, Biome Lifestyle

Bamboo is a strong, sustainable and fast-growing material, which has many advantages over comparable softwoods. The Bamboo Bulb vase is part of Biome Lifestyle's ever-expanding effort to make the most of this exciting material.
www.biomelifestyle.com

## Ahal vase, Biome Lifestyle

The classic looks of the Ahal vase, made in Spain from 100 percent post-consumer recycled glass, work equally well as a stand-alone piece or as a vessel in which to display flowers.
www.biomelifestyle.com

## Paperbag wastepaper baskets, Jos van der Meulen, Goods

These colourful wastepaper baskets are made from unused billboard posters that have been sewn together. It's always a surprise to see which poster has been used to make each Paperbag, even though you can often hardly recognize the advert. Paperbag comes in a flat package, for easy transportation and makes a wastepaper or tidy basket that will last for years.
www.josvandermeulen.nl

## Votives, Skoura

Skoura's Morrocan votives are made from either plain or painted reused metal cans, pierced with hundreds of tiny holes to allow the light to emanate through the metal.
www.skoura.co.uk

## Papier Mâché Sardine Bowl, Hen & Hammock

Handmade in a fairtrade environment in South Africa by women with HIV or AIDS, this lightweight papier maché bowl uses recycled sardine packaging.
www.henandhammock.co.uk

## Reclectic lanterns, Eco Outlet

Misprinted sheet metal and leftovers from aerosol production factories in India provide the colourful material for Eco Outlet's Reclectic lanterns.
www.ecoutlet.co.uk

## Translations waste bin, Eco Outlet

Created by a Thai artist fascinated with Japanese characters as graphic art, the Translation waste bin uses discarded magazines to create an exotic and environmentally friendly example of recycled materials being transformed into the very item they were once discarded into.
www.ecoutlet.co.uk

## Cake tin, Robert Archard

Robert Archard gives old tins a contemporary twist by sandblasting the existing paint and using a vinyl stencil to leave a graphic pattern behind.
www.robertarchard.com

### Aldente fruit and vegetable bowls, Moritz Böttcher and Holger de Boer

Made of 60 percent sawmill waste and 40 percent polypropylene, Aldente is a series of bowls for fruit and vegetables. Each nest-like bowl has a unique shape, as the material is shaped manually.
www.moritzboettcher.com

### Sisal baskets, Voodoo Blue

Voodoo Blue's hardwearing natural sisal baskets are handwoven in Kenya in a fairtrade women's cooperative.
www.voodooblue.co.uk

### Kiki Decorative vases, Perch!

Handmade in earthenware and finished with a non-toxic glaze, the Kiki can be used either as a large vase or as a simple decorative object.
www.perchdesign.net

## Authentics Magnetic Cork Board, The Conran Shop

Derived from sustainable sources, the cork in this board is harvested by hand every 12 to 14 years from trees that grow up to 200 years old.
www.conran.com

## Bambuster vases, Lidewij Spitshuis and Rixt Reitsma, We Made

A collaboration between Dutch designers and Indonesian crafts people, Bambuster is a series of vases made from pressed bamboo. The vases all feature a colour accent of rajut – a traditional style of Indonesian crochet.
www.lidewij.net
www.rixxt.nl

## Paperwork bowl, Hannah Lobley

Paperwork employ a unique method of recycling paper into a solid, wood-like material, which can be shaped using traditional woodworking techniques. Paperwork products also feature a unique pattern that resembles woodgrain.
www.hl-web.net

## Etsha Bowls, Patty Johnson, North South Project

Produced in collaboration with Botswana Craft and the Etsha Weavers, these handwoven baskets feature unique local patterns and are coloured with natural dyes.
www.northsouth
project.com

## Oval 3's vessels, Sarah Thirlwell

Sarah Thirlwell's beautiful organic vessels are produced from a mix of FSC graded birch plywood, vending cup plastic and yoghurt pot plastic.
www.sarahthirlwell.com

## Zomba baskets, Traidcraft

Traidcraft's Zomba baskets are woven from sustainable palm leaves in Malawi by Development Trading Limited, a fairtrade group established in 2000 to help disadvantaged workers in the area.
www.traidcraft.co.uk

### Garlic Queen basket, Thomas Eyck, Scholten & Baijings

Using traditional seventeenth-century Dutch basketry techniques, Thomas Eyck's Garlic Queen is woven from sustainable willow.
www.scholtenbaijings.com

### Salima palm baskets, Traidcraft

Fighting poverty through fairtrade practices, Traidcraft's Salima baskets are made from woven palm leaves in Malawi by the Mangochi Basket Weavers.
www.traidcraft.co.uk

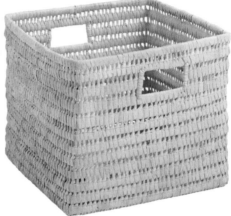

### Colour Rings napkin holders, Thomas Eyck, Scholten & Baijings

Reprising a seventeenth-century Dutch weaving technique, Thomas Eyck's napkin rings are woven from sustainable willow and feature tiny pieces of candy-coloured planed wood.
www.scholtenbaijings.com

## Bowls,
## David Trubridge, MOA

Carved from solid blocks of sustainable macrocarpa wood, David Trubridge's beautiful bowls reflect the designer's interest in modern computer technology synthesized with recurring natural patterns seen in Antarctica, Iceland and Australia.
www.davidtrubridge.com

## Serious Business basket,
## Thomas Eyck,
## Scholten & Baijings

Thomas Eyck's Serious Business basket takes traditional Dutch willow weaving techniques and combines them with futuristic looks and engineering.
www.scholtenbaijings.com

## Tierra Negra bowl,
## The Conran Shop

Handmade in the Andes of Colombia from nothing more than clay, Tierra Negra products can also be used as oven to tableware. Shaped by hand rather than being spun on a wheel, each piece is fashioned from coarse grey clay. Fine terracotta clay is then applied over the surface, followed by a coarse organic dust of dried grasses. The grasses burn rapidly as the vessels are fired resulting in the distinctive solid black finish.
www.conran.com

## Bol bowl, Woodloops

Woodloop's simple design, relies on the natural beauty of sustainable oak and is finished in natural, non-toxic oils.
www.woodloops.de

## Bol expanding fruitbowl, Christopher Metcalfe

Made in Australia from sustainably forested hoop-pine plywood, the Bol is a unique, expanding fruitbowl. To ensure minimum wastage of material, the parts used in the bowl's construction are tightly nested and then laser cut.
www.christophermetcalfe.com

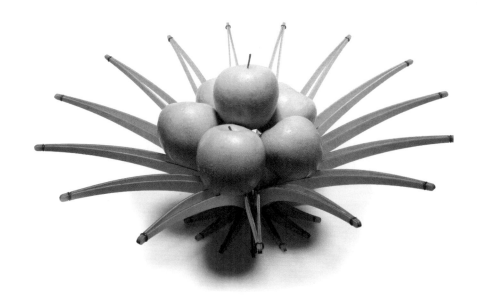

## Recycled glass bowl, Stephen Burks, Cappellini

'Cappellini Love' is a sustainable design project that Cappellini developed to protect the environment and support craftsmanship in countries with fragile economies. This bowl, made in collaboration with Stephen Burks, is crafted in Africa from recycled glass.
www.cappellini.it

### Rayon de Soleil dish, Tavie

Named after the central silver disc symbolizing the sun, the Rayon de Soleil dish is made from palm leaves in Niger by Touareg women working in rural cooperatives.
www.tavie.nl

### Recycled Glass Bowl, Massi

Fragments of recycled glass and ceramics are held in place with resin, creating an 'industrial' conglomerate in this eclectic design by Massi.
www.massi.it

### transNeomatic bowl, Humberto and Fernando Campana, Artecnica

The transNeomatic bowl is a collaborative, multifaceted testament to unconventional utilitarianism and radical recycling. Handcrafted from a used scooter tyre and natural wicker by skilled artisans in rural Vietnam, the product is an environmentally aware and socially conscious piece from concept to execution. In keeping with this theme, consumers are also encouraged to reuse the product's packaging – a bag made from recycled cotton, silk and linen thread.
www.artecnicainc.com

## Tennis Bowls,
## Pia Wallén, Arte & Cuoio

Avoiding the use of harmful chemicals, Arte &
Cuoio employ traditional nineteenth-century
tanning techniques to produce the leather used
in their distinctive, tennis-ball-like design.
www.artecuoio.com

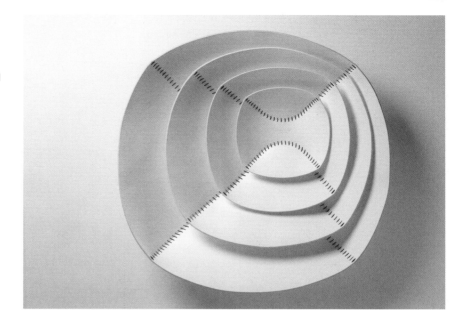

## Map Bowl,
## Bombus

Decorated in the muted pages of an iconic 1950s
London A to Z, Bombus' half-globe shaped bowl
is reinvented for the twenty-first century.
www.bombus.co.uk

### Eco Cooler,
### David Weatherhead,
### Designs We Need

The natural way to help root vegetables and fruit last longer, Eco Cooler is a handmade terracotta fruit bowl and vegetable store. Water poured into the bottom plate is absorbed by the terracotta. As the water evaporates it cools, helping to create the ideal cool, damp, dark environment to store potatoes, onions, garlic, swedes and other vegetables. The product is manufactured in Wales by a social enterprise called Crafts for Everyone which is engaged in employing and training people who are marginalized because of physical or mental disabilities.
www.dewene.com

### Basket Bowl,
### Perch!

Handmade in Brooklyn, New York, Perch! products are created using low-impact materials and processes. The earthenware Basket Bowl is finished in a non-toxic glaze and has a simple organic shape.
www.perchdesign.net

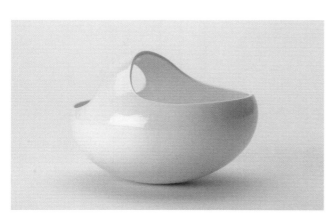

### MarbleWood Collection
### table settings,
### Todd Bracher, Mater

Using locally sourced hardwoods and black and white marble, the MarbleWood collection is produced by artisans in India's Jaipur Province. Using eight basic interchangeable components it is possible to create serving bowls, candleholders and candelabras from the collection.
www.materdesign.com

## Slush cast bowl, Ian McIntyre, Eco Age

Using recycled factory off-cuts, Ian McIntyre employs a unique process to capture the beauty and characteristics of pewter. The technique results in an unusual molten texture on the inside of each bowl, yet leaves the exterior smooth and shiny.
www.eco-age.com

## By Chance or By Design plates, Andreas Fabian

Andreas Fabian reuses the handles of antique garden tools on his fruit and vegetable plates. The unique handles provide a means of carrying his design and also link the vegetables back to the earth from which they came.
www.andreasfabian.eu

## 70cm Fruit, Ed Annink, Purple South

Cut from local, sustainably harvested timber in New Zealand, 70cm Fruit is a simple but unconventional fruit holder that is finished in natural oils and packaged in locally produced recycled cardboard.
www.purplesouth.com

## Potten Renske Papavoine containers, Nanimarquina

Made in India by Bhopal Rehabilitation, a fairtrade workshop that provides opportunities to those affected by the Bhopal disaster in 1984, Nanimarquina's delicate yet functional containers are made from a combination of reused multi-coloured fabrics covered with latex leather.
www.nanimarquina.com

## Beeswax Amphora, Tomás Gabzdil, Studio Libertiny

A conceptual design that addresses the ephemeral nature of commerce, Studio Libertiny's amphora is made of fragile beeswax in the form of an ancient Greek honey container. As the material itself is derived from pollen, Tomás Gabzdil decided to make a vase, in order to serve flowers on their 'last journey'.
www.studiolibertiny.com

## UNMADE 07 vase, Karen Ryan

In a comment about mass production and global branding, Karen Ryan takes unwanted porcelain vases and re-brands them by grinding off the surfaces but leaving her own UNMADE 07 logo. The vases have all been collected at car boot sales, charity shops, secondhand shops and jumble sales.
www.bykarenryan.co.uk

## Bojudo vase,
## Etel Carmona,
## One Eco Home

Carved in Brazil from 100 percent FSC certified breu wood, the Bojudo vase is helping to preserve the Amazon and Mata Atlantica Rainforests, which are threatened by destruction from cattle and soya producers, by contributing to responsible forest management. The vase is wrapped in a reusable blanket for transportation and finished with a natural, non-toxic oil to enhance the beauty of the wood.
www.oneecohome.co.uk

## Honeycomb Vase,
## Tomás Gabzdil,
## Studio Libertiny

Studio Libertiny's 'collaboration' with honeybees makes a statement about mass production by allowing nature to 'create' a manmade product. The vases are created by placing a basic beeswax mould printed with a honeycomb pattern into a beehive. The bees then do the rest.
www.studiolibertiny.com

## Paper Vase,
## Tomás
## Gabzdil,
## Studio
## Libertiny

The Paper Vase is created by forming 700 sheets of paper into a solid block and then turning this into a vase on a lathe. Each sheet of paper is printed with an identical image of a tree, creating a ghostly tree pattern on the surface of the vase. The project explores how paper – a product made from trees – can be returned to its original state and carved as if it were wood.
www.studiolibertiny.com

### Nesting Baskets, Bambu

Made from sustainable, 100 percent organically grown bamboo, these double-walled woven baskets are available in a wide range of shapes and sizes.
www.bambuhome.com

### In-Castro Collection leather boxes, Tim Toomey, Arte & Cuoio

Tanned using chestnut bark and mimosa, greased with animal fat and polished with amber, Arte & Cuoio use toxin-free, traditional nineteenth-century techniques to produce the In-Castro Collection, a range of leather boxes designed in various shapes and sizes.
www.artecuoio.com

### Beads & Pieces ceramic collection, Hella Jongerius, Artecnica

Beads & Pieces is a four-piece ceramic collection of startlingly delicate beading against robust black ceramic. With the help of Aid to Artisans, Artecnica offer an alternative means of employment to workers located in the primary coca leaf-growing region of Peru. The vessels are handcrafted by skilled Peruvian artisans, and feature traditional motifs from the Shipibo tribe.
www.artecnicainc.com

## Botanical Bark vases, Michael Aram

Taking inspiration from the natural world, and specifically forest forms and textures, Michael Aram's Botanical Bark vases are made completely out of polished recycled aluminium or copper. This playful rendering of white birch or cherry bark skilfully captures the delicacy and detail of the trees themselves.
www.michaelaram.com

## Milk Jug, Sheldon Cooney

Sheldon Cooney's Milk Jug is made by reheating and reforming milk bottles.
www.sheldoncooney.com

## Bowls, Roberta Amurri, Metacarta

Using recycled paper, Roberta Amurri creates products as light as paper and as hardy as rock. This is accomplished by using a core of existing secondhand structures, which are then covered with a humid paste of recycled paper. The resulting objects are extra-light, in spite of their monolithic appearance, and as solid, durable and practical as they look.
homepage.mac.com/robertaamurri

## Candleholder, Stephen Bretland, Twentytwentyone

Made using sustainably sourced wood, Stephen Bretland's Candleholder is part of Twentytwentyone's Ten exhibition, which proves that sustainable design can be creative, innovative, witty and, above all, desirable.
www.twentytwentyone.com

### Toy Mirror,
### Ryan McElhinney

Melding old toys together to create a mirror frame, Ryan McElhinney's fun design saves unwanted plastic from unnecessary landfill.
www.ryanmcelhinney.com

### Atlas Mirror,
### Bombus

Embracing the Victorian tradition of découpage, each Atlas Mirror is covered in pages from vintage atlases. The mirrors can be made to order and covered in maps from your own choice of location.
www.bombus.co.uk

### Mirror Mirror,
### Paul Loebach

Produced with a single laser cut which creates two mirrors from a slab of walnut, Mirror Mirror is a playful exploration of how efficient manufacturing processes can provide sustainable design solutions.
www.paulloebach.com

## Chatham Docks Mirror, Andy Wood

Constructed from reused timber salvaged from Chatham Docks, Andy Wood's simple mirror makes the most of the charm of antique wood, weathered by the elements for centuries.
www.andywood.eu

### Firefly wallhanging, Flexwood

Made from Flexwood, a sustainable, flexible wood veneer sheet, Firefly illustrates the versatility of this efficient and sustainable material.
www.flexwood.co.uk

### Log bowls, Doha Chebib, Loyal Loot Collective

Using unwanted waste wood from storms, development and re-landscaping, Doha Chebib has taken nature's leftovers and made these colourful eco-friendly bowls. Working with local crafts people, a tree is sliced into various lengths, and then turned by hand on a lathe until a smooth and even depression has been made. The dish of the bowl is hand-painted in a high-gloss acrylic and sealed with a water-based sealant. The smooth, glassy depression of the bowl complements the rustic bark base.
www.loyalloot.com

## Re Arita Porcelain, Minale-Maeda, Droog

Fired at a lower temperature and for a shorter time than traditional porcelain, Re Arita saves around 30 percent of energy compared with traditional manufacturing techniques.
www.droog.com

## Wall clock, Emiliano Godoy and Erika Hanson, Godoylab

Godoylab's simple clock design is constructed from sustainable Maplex®, an environmentally sound material. The clock is also designed for disassembly and biodegradation at the end of its life.
www.godoylab.com

## Added Value, By Louise

By fusing white earthenware butter-dish knobs and eggcups, embellished with floral decals, with plastic packaging By Louise makes the ordinary extraordinary. The Added Value range aspires to enhance how we view, use and understand everyday objects. The pieces aim to explore the issues of recycling while questioning the importance the mundane carries in our everyday lives.
www.by-louise.co.uk

## Wool Felt Garland, Sparrowkids

With the aim of encouraging interest in the environment, all Sparrowkids products are inspired by forms in nature. This method also results in timeless designs such as the Wool Felt Garlands, which are made from locally sourced sustainable and recycled fabrics. In addition, for every order a donation is made to the RSPB to protect Britain's sparrow population.
www.sparrowkids.co.uk

## Grandfather clock, Giles Miller

The ultimate simplification of grand antique furniture, Giles Miller's imaginative grandfather clock is made of cardboard, which is either sustainable or recycled.
www.gilesmiller.com

## Floating suspended objects, A4A Designs

Cut from sustainable recycled cardboard, the shapes in A4A Designs' Floating collection are inspired by undersea life and are designed to be suspended from the ceiling.
www.a4adesign.it

## Felt Rocks sculptural toys, Todd MacAllen and Stephanie Forsythe, Molo

Created as a by-product of making felt polishing wheels for optical lenses, Felt Rocks are 100 percent pure wool felt sculptural toys. They comprise entirely of material that would otherwise have been discarded. This is because small pieces of wool fluff become entangled with more and more felt fibre, growing like snowballs, as they tumble around a drum with the polishing wheels. Some are hand dyed with non-toxic dye, and others are left in natural shades of warm white and grey.
www.molodesign.com

## Pulp bulletin board, Umbra

Mounted on a frame of recyclable board, the Pulp bulletin board uses stacked black recycled paper to hold notes with or without pins.
www.umbra.com

## Alveole decorative CD case/picture, Studio Lo

A decorative CD case that also double as a mosaic-style picture, Alveole is produced from recycled card using energy efficient processes.
studio.lo.neuf.fr

### Grid wall-mounted organizer, Jaime Salm, Elizabeth Ingram, Mio

Made from die-cut and stitched recycled felt, Grid is a wall-mountable organizer with pockets, ideal for storing magazines, remote controls, books, pens and other small items. Made in the USA from locally sourced materials, all off-cuts are also recycled at the manufacturing facility.
www.mioculture.com

### Hand basket, Philip Luscombe

Developed through a study of how traditional materials and construction techniques might be appropriated in today's fast-moving consumer society, this basket highlights the energy and material mass used to make metal-cage shopping baskets. If this process were to be replaced with wicker weaving it could save a large amount of environmental damage.
philip-john.blogspot.com

### Recycled metal picture frames, Re-found Objects

Made from old oil drums, these recycled picture frames are hand crafted in a fair trade environment.
www.re-foundobjects.com

## Akasma glass baskets and trays, Satyendra Pakhalé, RSVP

Akasma is a collection of glass baskets and trays produced from reused architectural glass panels.
www.r-s-v-p.it

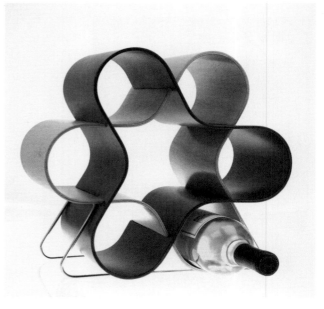

## Wine Knot wine rack, Scott Henderson, Mint Inc.

Using two intersecting pieces of sustainable birch and walnut plywood, the Wine Knot wine rack provides an efficient storage space for six regular-sized bottles and one oversized magnum or champagne bottle.
www.mintnyc.com

## Jordbro plant pot, Ikea

A plant pot that can be reversed to fit small or large plants, Jordbro is made from a mixture of recycled milk cartons and recycled material from the nappy industry.
www.ikea.com

## Garbino storage container, Umbra

The Garbino storage container is constructed from a mixture of recycled and corn-based plastics and is completely biodegradable.
www.umbra.com

## Decorative vessel, Frauke Stegmann, I Need Time To Think About Wildlife

As part of his 'I Need Time To Think About Wildlife' collections, Frauke Stegmann uses scraps of deconstructed waste materials and recycles them into unique decorative vessels, combining ceramic, plastic, leather and talisman-like decorative charms.
www.ineedtimetothinkaboutwildlife.org

## Suikerolifant decorative item, Bushglass

Bushglass is based at a craft centre opposite the Nairobi National Park, where over 50 people have been trained and now work, transforming recycled glass and scraps of other materials into decorative items such as the Suikerolifant. Profits are used to help the local area, and all packaging is secondhand.
www.kitengela-glass.com

## Flowerpot, Anne Black

Like all of Anne Black's porcelainware, these simple but elegant flowerpots are handcrafted in Vietnam in a fairtrade environment, and finished with a non-toxic glaze.
www.anneblack.dk

## Pebbles decorative objects, Woodloops

Made in sustainable oak or olive wood, Woodloops' pebbles are purely decorative items, which celebrate the simple beauty and rugged character of solid timber.
www.woodloops.de

## Pinch photo/ picture holder, Jos van der Meulen, Goods

Artist Jos van der Meulen collects wood from the forest floor and makes these small, unique objects, designed to hold a favourite photo or picture.
www.josvandermeulen.nl

## Card Capitals decorative letters, Re-found Objects

A range of decorative letters produced from recycled card, Card Capitals provide typographic charm and are weighted to stand up individually.
www.re-foundobjects.com

### Bulb vase, Esque Studio

Esque Studio produce all their beautiful glass products in two wind-powered electric furnaces which run three to four times more efficiently than traditional gas furnaces. 50 percent of their source material is recycled glass, and any waste materials are reused to produce their 'Eco Line'. www.esque-studio.com

### 2001: A Space Terrarium, Esque Studio

Produced in Esque Studio's low-energy studio, this terrarium is made using cutting-edge technology to reduce waste and gas consumption. In a lo-fi contrast to these high technologies, their products are also packed with biodegradable peanuts to keep them safe in transit. www.esque-studio.com

### Glass Drops, Re-found Objects

Re-found Objects' recycled Glass Drops can be suspended on strings around the house to provide pendulous decoration. www.re-foundobjects.com

## Flowers of Life Collection porcelain, Sebastian Menschhorn, Nymphenburg

The first porcelain manufacturer in Bavaria, all Nymphenburg porcelain is still hand-fashioned using the original water-powered kilns, which were engineering marvels of their times. In the Flowers of Life Collection, designer Sebastian Menschhorn has used traditional oriental designs that stand for growth, sensuality and wealth. By reducing single blossoms to linear drawings that are placed like large tattoos, his pieces carry a strong cultural message as much as an environmental one.
www.nymphenburg.com

## Candlestick, Helena Bancroft

Helena Bancroft's designs rework disused objects and give them a new lease of life by redefining their role and purpose. Made without disguising the products' original form – in this case cups and saucers – the new product becomes a respectful tribute to the old.
miss-helena@hotmail.co.uk

## Candelabra, Osian Batyka-Williams

After discovering that some restaurants replace their cutlery every nine months, Osian Batyka-Williams was compelled to reuse this useful raw material, imaginatively reworking the items into a candelabra.
www.osianbatykawilliams.com

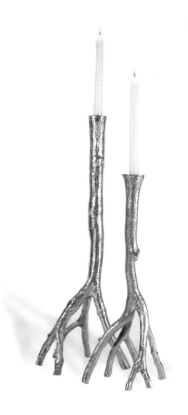

### Enchanted Forest candleholders, Michael Aram

Made entirely from recycled aluminium, Michael Aram's Enchanted Forest candleholders skilfully capture the forms and textures of the forest.
www.michaelaram.com

### Tendril Votive, Heath Nash

This sinuous votive features reused twisted wire and leaf shapes cut from discarded plastic bottles to create a delicate and organic candleholder.
www.heathnash.com

### TwoWay candleholder, Todd Bracher, Mater

Available in locally sourced black or white marble, Mater's TwoWay candleholder is crafted in a small, specialist factory by the skilled artisans of the Vishwakarma community in India.
www.materdesign.com

### Vintage Ceramic Votive, Kathleen Hills

Using reclaimed vintage glass shades from bric-à-brac shops and skips, Kathleen Hill reinterprets the familiar, placing it into a contemporary setting. Her range of products also incorporates packaging made from shredded waste paper.
www.kathleenhills.co.uk

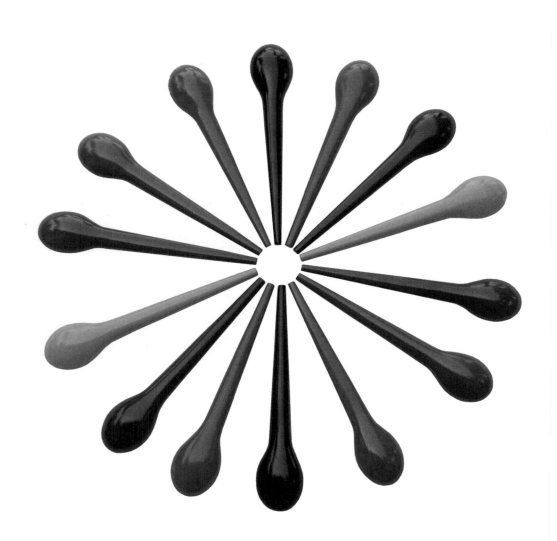

# Tableware

## Soupper Bowl, Rixt Reitsma and Lidewij Spitshuis, We Made

We Made is the result of a collaboration between Dutch designer's Rixt Reitsma and Lidewij Spitshuis, with the Indonesian Fair Trade organization, Apikri. The collection is inspired by a fusion of Dutch architecture and the local crafts on the island of Java.
www.lidewij.net
www.rixxt.nl

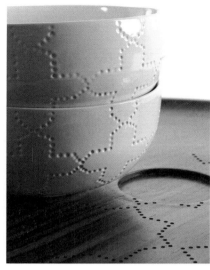

## Lacquerware bowls, Bambu

Marrying modern design with traditional bamboo craftsmanship, the Bambu Lacquerware collection is a certified organic, sustainable, fairtrade range of bowls, plates and other tabletop items. Each bowl is hand coiled with small strips of bamboo, shaped and finished with food-safe natural lacquer derived from the cashew nut tree. The result is a beautiful matt waterproof finish in a variety of warm colours.
www.bambuhome.com

## Eco Ware bowls, Tom Dixon

Made from bamboo fibre, the Eco Ware collection is fine enough for formal occasions and resilient enough both for outdoor and everyday use. After a long, functional life, these objects can be used as a plant pot, or simply composted.
www.tomdixon.net

## Natural Utensils, Bambu

Made in a fairtrade environment, Natural Utensils are hand-shaped from certified organic bamboo, and then burnished to a satiny feel. Stronger than wood, the utensils are guaranteed not to scratch cookware.
www.bambuhome.com

## Gemo Salad tongs, Ekobo

Handcrafted in a fairtrade environment using sustainable spun bamboo, these salad tongs are hand painted and wrapped in recycled packaging.
www.ekobo.org

## Tray, Ilio

This simple serving tray is constructed from sustainably sourced bamboo.
www.ilio.eu

## Bo bowls, Ekobo

With their super-glossy exterior and natural interior, each Ekobo product combines timeless design with an ethical way of working.
www.ekobo.org

## Egg-shaped bowl, Traidcraft

This hand-glazed ceramic bowl is made by a family-based pottery in rural Takul Nadu in India, whose work supports a local school.
www.traidcraft.co.uk

## Tilt Bowls, Anne Black

Anne Black's simple, classical pieces, such as these bowls, are finished with a non-toxic glaze.
www.anneblack.dk

## Global Service porcelain, Barnaby Barford, Nymphenburg

All Nymphenburg porcelain is hand fashioned using the factory's original water-powered kilns.
www.nymphenburg.com

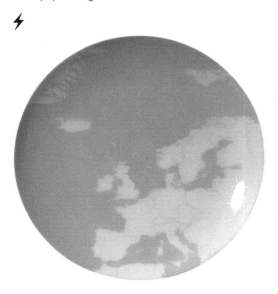

## Ceramic bowls, Feinedinge,

Feinedinge create modern sustainable ceramics fired in an electric kiln powered by hydroelectricity. These delicate porcelain bowls are handmade in Vienna.
www.feinedinge.at

## Uit de Klei Getrokken ('The Clay Drawn') tableware, Lonny van Rijswijck

The designer personally dug up the clay for her tableware from various parts of the Netherlands and fired it completely untreated and unglazed. The variety of textures and colours among the cups and saucers highlights the beauty and versatility of this completely natural material.
www.ateliernl.com

## InOut pitcher, Todd Bracher, Mater

Produced in a small, family-owned factory in the Gia Lam province of Vietnam, the porcelain InOut pitcher, with its removable lid, can be used for hot or cold beverages and is produced in a fairtrade environment.
www.materdesign.com

### Plates, Lou Rota

Lou Rota's work is all about reuse. She takes vintage and salvaged tableware and transforms it with photographic prints of flora and fauna.
www.lourota.com

### Reunified Floral Plates, Caroline Till

RCA graduate Caroline Till was presented with a BSI Sustainability Design Award in 2006. Her designs make use of secondhand and discarded materials, and she forges relationships with local manufacturers to source waste materials and seconds. These Reunified Floral Plates are designed to reduce landfill and incineration as well as reducing pressure on virgin resources.
caroline@carolinetill.com

### Black is Blue pitcher, Anne Black

Danish designer Anne Black engages a fairtrade workshop outside Hanoi in Vietnam with the challenging production of her handcrafted porcelain pieces, such as this elegant pitcher.
www.anneblack.dk

## Ryker plates, Lucy D.

Lucy D. recycles everyday china and turns it into 'silverware'. Founders Barbara Ambrosz and Karin Stiglmair source unwanted china of various ages sizes and forms and then unify the pieces into a new set of tableware by applying a simple graphic element. Each edge of a plate is glazed by hand with platinum, then re-fired, leaving only a central square section of the original plate visible.
www.lucyd.com

## Salvation Stacks tableware, Laurene Leon Boym, Boym Partners

Previously produced by Moooi, Salvation Stacks give a new life to mismatched plates and cups doomed to eternal oblivion and neglect. Assembled into large and sumptuous compositions, the stacks become part tableware, part sculpture.
www.boym.com

## Nymphenburg Sketches porcelain ware, Hella Jongerius, Nymphenburg

The beautiful Nymphenburg Sketches collection brings together animal and plant designs from the company's history, illustrating the process of creation that each design goes through.
www.nymphenburg.com

### Teacup and saucer, Frauke Stegmann, I Need Time To Think About Wildlife

As part of his 'I Need Time To Think About Wildlife' series, Frauke Stegmann brings together mismatched teacups and saucers and unites them with scribbled glaze.
www.ineedtimetothinkaboutwildlife.org

### Reunified Blob Plates, Caroline Till

Inspired by the contrast between contemporary and traditional, low tech, hi-tech, the painterly and the graphic, Caroline Till seeks to reinvent objects that might otherwise be discarded. The designer sources china from charity shops and re-patterns individual pieces to re-unify collections. The Reunified Blob Plates are designed to reduce landfill and incineration as well as reducing pressure on virgin resources.
caroline@carolinetill.com

### Classic Handmade Mug, Traidcraft

Traidcraft's Classic Handmade Mugs are made by Craft Link, an organization that helps craft groups in Vietnam to improve their livelihoods. Its goals include cultural preservation, income generation for small Vietnamese artisans and acquiring new markets in a changing economy. Artisans working with Craft Link receive tools, interest-free loans, education, training and literacy classes.
www.traidcraft.co.uk

## SoftBowls, Jaime Salm and Roger Allen, Mio

SoftBowls are decorative bowls made from 100 percent moulded wool. Manufactured in Philadelphia by one of the last remaining millineries in the US, each container is handmade by local craftspeople. The design requires less than one tenth of the energy needed to make comparable ceramic products. www.mioculture.com

## New/Old Tea Sets, Christine Misiak

Christine Misiak mixes an element of craft with recycled industrially manufactured products. She rejuvenates neglected tea sets, by recycling, restyling and resurfacing them, transforming them into elegant one-off pieces that are a celebration of the past and present. www.christinemisiak.co.uk

## Recycled Misiak Doilies, Christine Misiak

Christine Misiak reinvents unwanted objects found in junk shops and brings them back to life. This collection features a mixture of old crocheted cotton doilies injected with a burst of colour. www.christinemisiak.co.uk

## Tasses drinking glasses, Regis R

Regis R mixes recycled glassware with cable and wire to form handled drinking glasses.
r.egis.online.fr

## Citi Group goblets, Bribe

Australian glass company Bribe use recycled glass to create their range of goblets etched with iconic city skylines.
www.bribeint.com

## Piece of Tin milk jug and sugarbowl, Lianne van Genugten

A tin is more than just packaging for food; Lianne van Genugten thinks it's a product with character and wants to breathe new life into it. Made from recycled tins, her products are made by hand under fairtrade conditions by people in Tanzania, giving each piece its own characteristics.
www.liannevangenugten.nl

## Rustic recycled glasses, John Lewis

The John Lewis Rustic collection is made in Spain from recycled glass. Urban waste glass is collected and recombined. The process helps conserve energy and materials and produces glass with a subtle green tinge.
www.johnlewis.com

## Carafe and glasses, Esque Studio

Part of Esque Studio's beautiful and innovative Eco collection, these recycled string-bound carafe and glasses are produced using waste glass in wind-powered electric furnaces, which run three to four times more efficiently than traditional gas furnaces.
www.esque-studio.com

## Recycled glassware, Traidcraft

Made from recycled glass, Traidcraft's simple and stylish jugs and wine glasses are produced under fairtrade conditions in Bolivia.
www.traidcraft.co.uk

### Dutch Wood chopping boards, Lotte Van Laatum, Tuttobene

Based on the geographical shape of the region in the Netherlands in which the wood grew, Dutch Wood chopping boards are made from timber managed by the Dutch Forestry Council. The trees are only allowed to be harvested when it is necessary for the wellbeing of the forest as a whole.
www.tuttobene.nl

### Haute Surface ZigZag Set, Jaime Salm, Mio

These interlocking cork trivets are inspired by railroad tracks and are entirely sustainable and recyclable. They fit together in many ways to create table mats, table runners and even mouse mats.
www.mioculture.com

### Haute Surface Houndstooth Set, Jaime Salm, Mio

Made from reconstituted cork, Houndstooth interlocking cork trivets are inspired by patterns in clothing design. The trivets are sustainable and recyclable and can be arranged into table runners, trivets or placemats.
www.mioculture.com

## Trivet Set, Cork Nature

Made using FSC certified cork, the Trivet Set is fully recyclable.
www.corknature.com

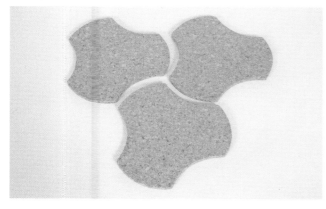

## Place mat, Cork Nature

Cork Nature's place mats are made using FSC certified cork and are fully recyclable.
www.corknature.com

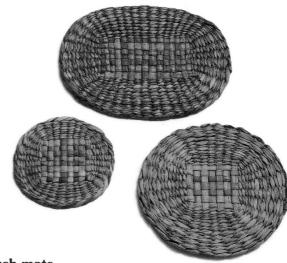

## News Mats, Re-found Objects

Re-found Objects' colourful News Mats are made from coiled pieces of recycled newspapers.
www.re-found objects.com

## Rush mats, Felicity Irons, Rush Matters

Felicity Irons handcrafts traditional rush products from English bulrush, using no chemical treatments at any time during the harvest or in the weaving of the final designs. Each 100 percent natural mat is extremely long-lasting yet also biodegradable at the end of its life.
www.rushmatters.co.uk

## Roster Bamboo Plates, Rixt Reitsma and Lidewij Spitshuis, We Made

We Made is the result of a collaboration between Dutch designer's Rixt Reitsma and Lidewij Spitshuis, with the Indonesian Fair Trade organization Apikri. Their Roster Bamboo Plates are inspired by a fusion of Dutch architecture and the local crafts on the island of Java.
www.lidewij.net
www.rixxt.nl

## Cutting Boards, Bambu

The producers of Bambu's certified organic sustainable bamboo cutting and serving boards are organized as a fairtrade collective, and all packaging is also made from FSC certified sources or 100 percent post-consumer recycled fibres. In addition, more than one percent of net sales are donated to the preservation and restoration of the natural environment.
www.bambuhome.com

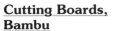

## Tapestry Tray, Frédérique Morrel

Based on the reworking of vintage needlework found in secondhand shops and jumble sales, Frédérique Morrel's Tapestry Tray gives subversive new meaning to tapestries that once took hours to make.
www.frederiquemorrel.com

### Leaf Plate,
### Ganesha

Made from sal and siali leaves, from the forests of Orissa in eastern India, Ganesha's fairtrade Leaf Plates are completely biodegradable.
www.ganesha.co.uk

### Tapered Bowl,
### Liam O'Neill, David Mellor

Liam O'Neill is one of Ireland's leading wood-turners, and only uses only timber from trees felled through old age or storm damage. The quality of his bowls lies in their subtle detailing as well as the intrinsic beauty of the wood.
www.davidmellordesign.com

### Cork Bowls,
### Simon Mount, Doistrinta

Promoting sustainability by using cork, Doistrinta's bowls are hardwearing, waterproof and sustainable.
www.designfactory.org

## Tempo platter, Ekobo

These platters are hand crafted in a fairtrade environment using sustainable spun bamboo. They are then hand painted and wrapped in recycled packaging.
www.ekobo.org

## Sushi board, The Pfeifer Consultancy

The Pfeifer Consultancy's sushi board consists of three components: a stainless steel tray and two solid timber plates that are made from sustainable rubber wood – a waste product of the rubber industry.
www.leonhardpfeifer.com

## Solidware collection, Bambu

The Solidware collection of trays, bowls and utensils are made of certified organic bamboo laminates. The range is 'carbonized' to a rich golden brown, which means that the bamboo is oven-baked and involves no stains, dyes or toxins. The producers use only water-based formaldehyde-free adhesives and all products are hand sanded and finished using a food-safe oil produced from vegetable oils and waxes.
www.bambuhome.com

## All-Occasion Veneerware® single-use plates, Bambu

Made from sustainably harvested, certified organic bamboo, All-Occasion Veneerware® is Bambu's answer to the paper plate. A single-use collection of bamboo plates and utensils, the pieces are ideal for picnics, weddings and parties and will biodegrade in four to six months in a compost heap. Bambu has also been granted the Co-op America Seal of Approval for commitment towards fair treatment of workers, promoting healthy communities, preserving the environment and providing quality products. www.bambuhome.com

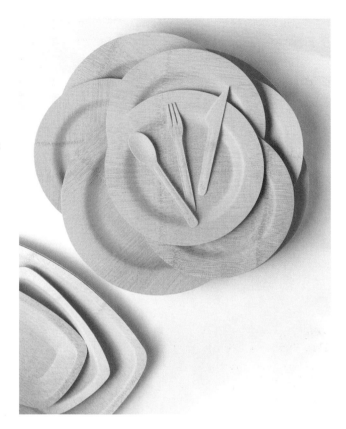

## Bowl, Cork Nature

Cork Nature uses FSC certified cork to make products in harmony with nature. The cork oak is a slow-growing tree that lives for up to 200 years, which allows it, on average, to be stripped 16 times during its lifetime. The first stripping takes place after 25 years with the subsequent ones carried out every nine years. Cork Nature ensure that trees are stripped ethically and responsibly. Any waste produced during the process is also recycled. www.corknature.com

# Walls & Floors

### Kitchenset wall covering, Dominic Crinson

Printed with non-toxic water-based UV-resistant inks, Dominic Crinson's psychedelic designs will remain bright throughout their lifetime. The wall covering is easy to remove in entire strips and can even be reused when you move house.
www.crinson.com

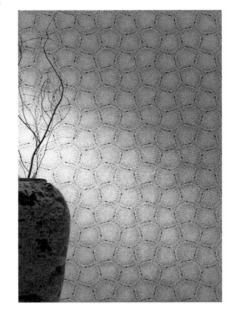

### Terrashella 7 wall covering, Dominic Crinson

Like all Crinson's wall coverings, this one, from the Terrashella Collection, is made from a durable blend of textile fibres and cellulose from FSC certified forests
www.crinson.com

### Urban Birdcage wallpaper, Asma Hussain, Graham & Brown

These environmentally friendly wallpapers are printed using water-based dye on paper from 100 percent FSC-managed sources. Asma Hussain's design focuses on the loss of many species of birds to urbanization. The motif combines the form of a traditional birdcage with urban architectural influences. Each roll is packaged in compostable materials made from corn.
www.graham brown.com

### Rainforest wallpaper, Jennifer Vargas, Graham & Brown

The Rainforest wallpaper design has been heavily influenced by Jennifer Vargas' Latin American heritage. She used vibrant colours and exotic patterns, and the paper seeks to capture the essence of her homeland.
www.graham brown.com

## Fearn wall hanging, Ninette van Kamp

Artist Ninette van Kamp delicately cuts vintage wallpaper to create beautiful and intricate wall hangings.
www.textilefutures.co.uk

## Wallpaper tiles, Celia Suzanne Sluijter

Handmade in a fairtrade environment in Nepal, Celia Suzanne Sluijter's ricepaper wall coverings embrace the traditional culture, materials and techniques of the women who make them. Designed to be arranged in a grid formation, the tiles are printed using natural, non-toxic dyes in leaf, flower or hand-shaped designs.
www.celia.nl

## Shuffle wallpaper, Dominic Crinson

This non-toxic, recyclable and sustainable wallpaper, from the Ensemble Collection, features linear geometric patterns. Fluid brush strokes are mapped across organic layers.
www.crinson.com

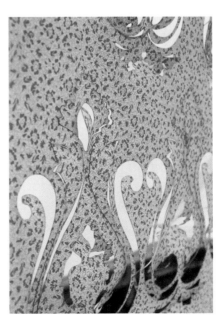

## Lace wallpaper, Ninette van Kamp

Artist Ninette van Kamp, delicately cuts vintage wallpaper to create beautiful and intricate wall hangings
www.textilefutures.co.uk

## Wallpapers, Louise Body

Featured designs, clockwise from top left, are: Pavilion Birds, Flower Press; Floral; Harry's Garden. Louise Body wallpapers are eco-friendly, using water-based inks and no hazardous solvents. The chlorine-free paper is sourced from managed forests where growth exceeds cut volume and any waste from wallpaper trimming is recycled.
www.louisebody wallprint.com

### Junglish wall covering, Dominic Crinson

Dominic Crinson's non-woven wall covering is breathable yet washable and, being made from 100 percent textile fibres and cellulose derived from FSC certified forests, contains no substances that are damaging to the health or the environment. www.crinson.com

### Fossil wallpaper, Andrea Sallee, Graham & Brown

This Fossil wallpaper highlights the simple natural beauty found in ancient fossil footprints, while drawing attention to the question of the footprint this generation will leave on our world. www.graham brown.com

### Wall covering, Asma Hussain

Asma Hussain works with natural wool and felt insulation to encourage the re-use of materials and household products. This bespoke wall covering range is inspired by the history of fabricated homes and shelters, alongside the history of wallpaper, tapestries and heating systems. The pieces highlight awareness of over-consumption within the home by addressing the potential of thermal insulation and how 'dressing' a wall as a means of decoration can reduce waste. www.asmahussain.com

### Lotos 1, Dominic Crinson

This non-woven wall covering is from the Essence Collection. It is breathable yet washable and, being made from 100 percent textile fibres and cellulose derived from FSC certified forests, it contains no substances that are damaging to the health or the environment. www.crinson.com

## Beauty wallpaper, Graham & Brown

Printed on paper from managed timber sources that are FSC certified, and printed using water-based inks that contain no VOCs or solvents, Beauty is a twist on traditional florals combined with hand-printed classic scroll work. Each roll is packaged in a compostable material made from corn starch.

www.grahambrown.com

## Summer wallpaper, Graham & Brown

Printed on paper from managed timber sources that are FSC certified and printed using water-based inks that contain no VOCs or solvents, Summer is a simple hand-block effect floral wallpaper.

www.grahambrown.com

## Aspen wallpaper, Graham & Brown

This striped leaf pattern is printed on paper from managed timber sources that are FSC certified and printed using water-based inks that contain no VOCs or solvents. The wallpaper is packaged in a compostable material made from corn starch.

www.grahambrown.com

## Peony wallpaper, Graham & Brown

A modern floral design demonstrating the vibrancy found in nature, Peony is printed on paper from managed timber sources that are FSC certified and printed using water-based inks that contain no VOCs or solvents. The wallpaper is packaged in a compostable material made from corn starch.

www.grahambrown.com

## The Bittern wallpaper, Jo Angell, Graham & Brown

The bittern, whose reed-bed habitats are under threat from rising sea levels, forms the inspiration for Jo Angell's wallpaper design. There are only fifty breeding pairs of bitterns left in the whole of the UK, an indication of environmental changes in today's world. Using elements of the bird's feather patterns alongside textural influences from its habitat, Jo Angell has created beautiful and thought-provoking wallpaper.
www.grahambrown.com

## Nature wallpaper, Graham & Brown

A natural textured-block design, Nature is printed on paper from managed timber sources that are FSC certified and printed using water-based inks, which contain no VOCs or solvents.
www.grahambrown.com

## Spring wallpaper, Graham & Brown

Inspired by the wild and untamed beauty of an English cottage garden in spring, this wallpaper is printed on paper from managed timber sources that are FSC certified and printed using water-based inks, which contain no VOCs or solvents.
www.grahambrown.com

## Heritage wallpaper, Graham & Brown

Inspired by age-old traditional hand-blocked damasks, Heritage is printed on paper from managed timber sources that are FSC certified and printed using water-based inks, which contain no VOCs or solvents.
www.grahambrown.com

## Palm Panel wall covering, Omarno

Omarno's handmade Palm Panel combines texture, warmth, originality and beauty, to create a completely biodegradable and sustainable wall covering made from natural coconut shell.
www.omarno.com

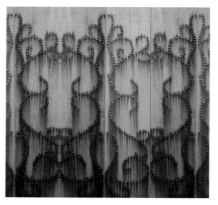

## Come Rain or Shine wall covering, Heather Smith

Come Rain or Shine works in conjunction with the natural elements – allowing nature itself to bring pattern and decoration to different surfaces. Here, Heather Smith embellishes reclaimed oak and birch with studded metal patterns then leaves the pieces outside at the mercy of the elements. The result is an organic decoration without harm to the environment.
www.heathersmithcollection.com

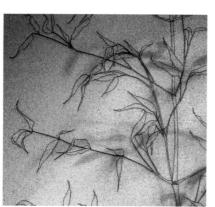

## Bamboo Cork wall covering, Sam Pickard

Created either as a customized panel or designed for a specific site, Sam Pickard's visually intriguing Bamboo Cork wall covering features sustainable cork, laser-etched with elegant graphic bamboo imagery.
www.sampickard.co.uk

## Bespoke wallpaper, Catherine Hammerton

Catherine Hammerton creates bespoke wallpaper panels by layering vintage wallpapers and fabrics. The pieces are designed to suit the clients' individual needs and unique aesthetic and can feature anything from delicate cut-out birds and flowers to repeat stitched patterns.
www.catherinehammerton.com

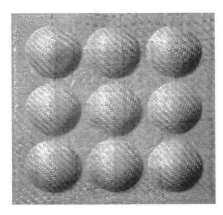

## Moboo wall panel, Satyendra Pakhalé

Satyendra Pakhalé's bamboo wall panel combines age-old craft traditions with contemporary design. He addresses the many issues with the bamboo trade, ensuring that he only sources fairly traded sustainable bamboo without damaging panda habitats.
www.satyendra-pakhale.com

## Acoustic Weaves PaperForms wall covering, Jaime Salm, Mio

Made from 100 percent post- and pre-consumer waste paper, Mio's PaperForms offer a new concept in surface coverings, offering the ability to customize and redefine a space.
www.mioculture.com

## V2 PaperForms wall covering, Jaime Salm, Mio

These lightweight recycled modules can be installed temporarily with tape or permanently with wallpaper paste. They come in packs of 12 and can be mixed and matched to customize a space on a budget.
www.mioculture.com

## Vintage wallpaper, Claire Coles

Claire Coles offers a tactile new approach to wallpaper design. Stitching vintage wallpapers of various textures and patterns together, she creates one-off intricate and ethereal papers, illustrations and accessories.
www.clairecolesdesign.co.uk

## Flow PaperForms wall covering, Jaime Salm, Mio

These lightweight tiles nest closely together and can cover as much or as little of a wall as required. The unique modular structure also means that any damaged tiles can easily be replaced.
www.mioculture.com

## Twig Wall Panel, Pinch

Made from sustainable solid ash forest thinnings, the Twig Wall Panel is fixed to a plywood board, neatly bringing the charm of the forest into the home.
www.pinchdesign.com

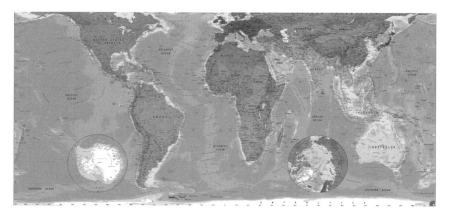

## Future Map mural, Future Mapping Company, Digitile

Future Mapping Company's modern redesign of the Cylindrical Equal Area Projection is exquisitely rendered on a mixture of textile fibres and cellulose derived from FSC certified forests, to make an impressive wall or floor mural.
www.digitile.co.uk

### Horizon screen, Dylan Freeth, MARK

Taking its name from the wide, distant horizons of Cornwall's north coast, Dylan Freeth's sustainable oak screen provides privacy while also allowing plenty of light to penetrate, keeping a sense of space.
www.markproduct.com

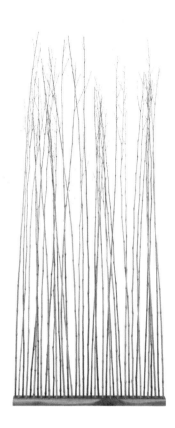

### Cendani screen, Habitat

Made of sustainable bamboo with a teak base, Habitat's screen provides a natural room divider.
www.habitat.co.uk

### Esteira Screen, One Eco Home

Turn one space into two with the Esteira screen, an organic rippling design made from 100 percent FSC certified Brazilian freijo wood. The forest stewardship of freijo contributes to the preservation of Brazil's precious rainforests.
www.oneecohome.co.uk

## Softwall temporary wall, Stephanie Forsythe and Todd MacAllen, Molo

Softwall belongs to Molo's family of expandable and compressible honeycomb structures called Soft. The wall creates the opportunity to shape more intimate, ephemeral space within larger open spaces in a temporal way, and then give that space back to the larger room when needed. Available in three materials, including recycled lightweight tissue paper and recycled craft paper, all the versions are surprisingly hardwearing and 100 percent recyclable. www.molodesign.com

## Fluted Screen, Giles Miller, Farm Designs

Giles Miller's Fluted Screen demonstrates the designer's idea of alternating the angle of the corrugation in cardboard to produce different shades and decorative patterns upon the surface of the recycled cardboard. www.gilesmiller.com

## Piasa room divider, Godoylab

The Piasa is part of Godoylab's knitted furniture family. Its name comes from an Illini legend telling the story of the Piasa bird, a huge mythical creature covered in scales. The pieces are joined in such a way that they can freely rotate to create different profiles. This scaled room divider made from sustainable materials can be manufactured in any length. www.godoylab.com

## Paperback Partition, Lucy Jane Norman

The Paperback Partition uses thousands of waste books, which would otherwise end up in landfill, to create an interesting room divider that also provides good heat and acoustic insulation. The partition uses an existing structure from Avanti Systems and the books can be installed in varying styles and patterns.
www.lucynorman.co.uk

## BioWall space divider, Rachel Wingfield, Loop

BioWall uses living plants to create a space divider, which can be used inside or out. With plants creeping and crawling around the structure, BioWall can become an indoor, living hedge that divides space and improves the air. The basic frame is a hand woven, three-dimensional structure that can be crafted into lace-like walls of any dimension.
www.loop.ph

## Nomad System, Jaime Salm, Roger Allen, Mio

Made from recycled, double-wall cardboard, the Nomad System is an architectural system that can be assembled into free-standing sculptural screens, temporary partitions, rooms or even displays, without hardware, tools or damage to existing structures. Made from recycled craft paper, the easily reconfigurable and replaceable modules provide a low impact alternative to temporary walls.
www.mioculture.com

## Low VOC paint, Little Greene Paint Company

Made with the finest materials, all Little Greene's paints are manufactured in the company's factory in the foothills of Snowdonia. Containing minimal VOCs, the water-based paint has excellent coverage, meaning that a room can be painted in significantly fewer coats. The knock-on effect of this is that fewer tins need to be delivered and so transportation pollution is reduced. Little Greene also use recycled materials to make their tins.
www.thelittlegreene.com

## Farrow & Ball collection

Farrow & Ball's edited palette of historic colours continues to use natural ingredients such as linseed oil and China clay and avoids the use of harmful ingredients such as ammonia and formaldehyde. The VOC levels for their Estate Emulsion, Modern Emulsion and Exterior Masonry paints are so low that these finishes are classified as 'Zero VOC' by the US Environmental Protection Agency standards. The companies traditional tin packaging also has a high recycled content and is easily recyclable.
www.farrow-ball.com

## Pots of Paint collection, Edward Bulmer, Aglaia

With a background in architectural history and interior design, Edward Bulmer is ideally placed to select a palette of 50 paint colours that work equally well in old or new houses. The collection, called Pots of Paint, is mixed by Aglaia and made from entirely natural ingredients, without solvents or VOCs. The paints have a wonderfully chalky finish, smell delicious and let walls breathe naturally.
www.aglaiapaint.com

## Siecle paint

A high-quality household paint available in a range of hard-to-find modernist colours, Siecle Paint is manufactured in a wind-powered factory.
www.sieclecolours.com

## Auro paints and wood finishes

Based on plant and mineral pigments, Auro paints and wood finishes are completely organic, and allow walls to breathe naturally. Available in a variety of finishes, including a soft, super-matt emulsion, a hardwearing washable emulsion, silk, eggshell, gloss and powdered casein paint, the products are ideally suited to allergy sufferers or those who are chemically sensitive. Auro were officially accredited as a Carbon neutral manufacturer in 2006.
www.auro.co.uk

## Marston & Langinger Paint

Formulated to tackle the environmental issues associated with most paints on the market, Marston & Langinger's premium water-based paints contain no chemical solvents and are non-toxic. The paints are also non-flammable, low carbon, and, when dry, are perfectly safe for children and pets. They also have the longest life of equivalent paints on the market.
www.marston-and-langinger.com

## Nutshell Natural Paints

Nutshell Natural Paints are 100 percent ecological, and are made from natural raw materials that offer a radical alternative to commercial paints manufactured with vinyl resins and petrochemical solvents. The paints are completely carbon neutral and allergen free. With no toxic fumes, rooms can be painted and then slept in on the same day, making the paints totally safe for children's rooms. The paints are also microporous, allowing surfaces to breathe and so protecting the fabric of the building.
www.nutshellpaints.com

## Biofa paints and varnishes, The Green Building Store

Biofa is a range of high-performance natural paints and varnishes that provide an environmentally friendly alternative to conventional paints. The range includes interior flat emulsion, kitchen and bathroom paints, gloss and eggshell finishes, flooring waxes and oils.
www.greenbuildingstore.co.uk

## Osmopot colour finishes, The Green Building Store

Osmopot colour finishes are based solely on natural oils and waxes. Unlike synthetic finishes, natural oils and waxes penetrate into wood, keeping it healthy and elastic while preventing it from becoming dry and brittle. They are also microporous, allowing natural moisture movement and reducing shrinking or swelling of the timber. www.greenbuilding store.co.uk

## Ecos Paint

Ecos' solvent-free paints and varnishes are entirely non-toxic, VOC-free, solvent-free and at least 7,000 times purer than the EU 2010 regulations demand. Ecos paint is available in a range of 108 co-ordinated colours, including colour groups such as Shaker, California and Cotswold. The company also offers a unique colour matching service. www.ecospaints.com

### The White Horse rug, Annie Sherburne Designs

Inspired by the natural world, Annie Sherburne's rugs are handmade using sustainable materials and dyed with natural plant dyes.
www.anniesherburne.co.uk

### Sea Trout rug, Claesson Koivisto Rune, Märta Måås-Fjetterström AB

Swedish architects and designers Mårten Claesson, Eero Koivisto and Ola Rune designed this rug, inspired by sound patterns. The rugs are produced entirely by hand from 100 percent wool on a warp of flax.
www.claesson-koivisto-rune.se

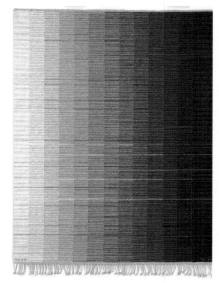

### Broadband rug, Claesson Koivisto Rune, Märta Måås-Fjetterström AB

Designed by architects Claesson Koivisto Rune, the Broadband rug is inspired by computer technology. The yarn is naturally coloured in the company's own dye house, situated in the basement of the weaving studio.
www.claesson-koivisto-rune.se

### Satellite carpet, Claesson Koivisto Rune, Märta Måås-Fjetterström AB

This hand-woven carpet was inspired by the spectogram and is naturally coloured.
www.claesson-koivisto-rune.se

## Aladin carpet, Tramando, Design Connection Argentine Group

The Aladin carpet is handmade by crocheting recycled materials from the textile industry.
www.tramando.com

## Silence rug, Permafrost

Created by Norwegian design quartet Permafrost, the Silence rug is handmade from 100 percent sustainable New Zealand wool. At first glance, the rug gives an impression of glistening white snow – a common sight in freezing Norway – then you discover the small tracks left by a passing hare.
www.permafrost.no

## John Deere rug, Permafrost

The John Deere rug offers a snapshot of life in rural Scandinavia. Heavy machinery has long-since replaced the labour of farm animals, leaving its trademark tracks in the grass and mud. The rug is handmade from 100 percent sustainable New Zealand wool.
www.permafrost.no

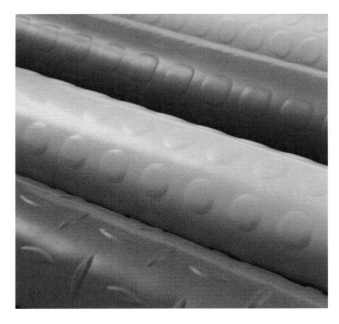

## DalNaturel rubber flooring, Dalsouple

It is a common misconception that modern rubber flooring is a 'natural' product. In fact, virtually all the rubber flooring on the market today is made from synthetic SBR, a petrochemical by-product. By contrast, Dalsouple's DalNaturel contains over 90 percent natural ingredients, with all the rubber content being completely natural. Natural rubber is a wholly renewable raw material, and mature rubber trees are exceptionally efficient at absorbing carbon dioxide from the atmosphere. Rubber can also be recycled not just once, but several times over.
www.dalsouple.co.uk

## Aluminium flooring, Alulife

Available in a variety of colours and finishes, Alulife's brilliantly space-age recycled aluminium flooring is laid using a technique similar to that of traditional floors, ensuring that the finished surface is perfectly flat, smooth and even.
www.alulife.com

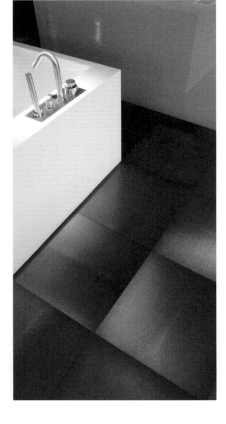

## Carpet, Orken Oliven, 2form Design

All 2form designs are produced in India on fairtrade terms. The carpets are made of 100 percent natural wool, cotton and silk, which are dyed with only natural pigments. Waste is recycled back into production of felt or threads, and all products are transported by sea with minimal packaging.
www.2form.no

## Recycled cardboard boxes, Wendy Plomp

The thinking behind Wendy Plomp's recycled cardboard boxes really does come from 'outside the box'! With ornate, arabesque-like patterns printed on their interior surfaces, when deconstructed the boxes can be laid on the floor as unconventional rugs.
www.wnd.nu

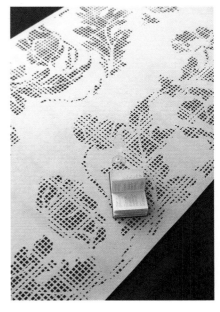

## Rubber rug, Annemette Beck

Annemette Beck's rugs and runners are woven of recycled bicycle tyres, cables and cotton warp.
www.annemette-beck.dk

## Memento rug, 2form Design

Made of 100 percent wool felt, the Memento rug is cut using a water jet. This method is safe, clean and environmentally friendly as no gases or vapours are generated. The waste from cutting the rug is recycled back into producing more felt, and the water used is recycled elsewhere in the factory.
www.2form.no

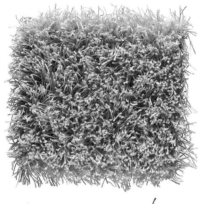

## Fogg rug, Gunilla Lagerhem Ullberg, Kasthall

An elegant long-pile rug made from 100 percent linen, Fogg is available to buy in a variety of naturally dyed colours.
www.kasthall.com

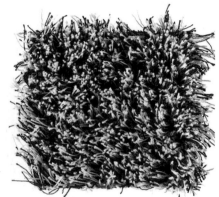

## Pebble rug, Ksenia Movafagh, 2form Design

The Pebble rug is produced in India under fair trade conditions from 100 percent wool. The wool is neither dyed nor bleached and is washed with only toxin-free soap. The rug is also recyclable.
www.2form.no

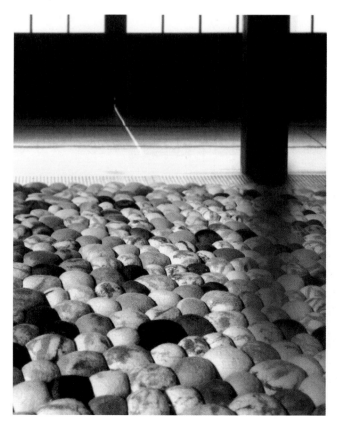

### DNA Soft Cobbles rug, Annie Sherburne Designs

Constructed entirely from organic felted wool balls, Annie Sherburne's architectural fabrics are made from the naturally washed and carded fleeces of British sheep. They are produced in a range of colours, depending on availability from the latest shearing.
www.anniesherburne.co.uk

### Abha carpet, Jacaranda

Jacaranda create natural broadloom carpets made from 100 percent sustainable undyed wool. Their traditional wooden looms are hand operated, with no need for electricity, and although designed to last, the carpets can easily be recycled at the end of their lives.
www.jacarandacarpets.com

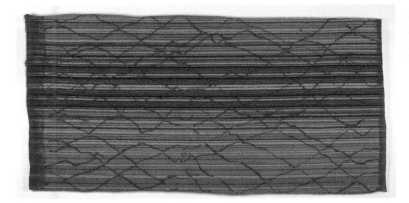

### Scheer rug, Stefan Scholten and Carol Baijings, Scholten & Baijings

The unpredictability of using remnants from the carpet-making industry is exploited in Scholten & Baijings' Scheer rug.
www.scholtenbaijings.com

## Deken rug, Stefan Scholten and Carol Baijings, Scholten & Baijings

Remnants and supplementary material from carpet-making is recycled in the production of the Deken rug. This material has the same high quality as the main product, but its size, colour and pile height differs each time. This unpredictability is embraced in the Deken rug.
www.scholtenbaijings.com

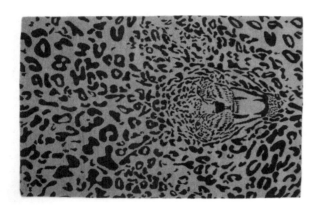

## Animal rug, Themselves

Themselves' hand-tufted rugs are created in collaboration with Alain Rouveure, who has been working with Tibetan village communities in the Himalayas since the 1970s to produce fairtrade, handcrafted goods without using child labour or harmful chemicals. Customers are given photographs of their rug being made and the name of the individual craftsman responsible.
www.alainrouveure.com

## Pink Rose Rug, Celia Suzanne Sluijter

Celia Suzanne Sluijter's aim is to alleviate poverty and improve production methods in the area where her products are made; in this case Nepal and Tibet.
www.celia.nl

## Orchid rug,
## Celia Suzanne Sluijter

Embracing the traditional techniques of Nepali and Tibetan carpet knotting, Celia Suzanne Sluijter's raw silk rugs are produced under fairtrade conditions by a production company founded by a Tibetan refuge.
www.celia.nl

## Tatamata rug,
## Soejima

Soejima's Tatamata rug is made of woven igusa, a plant-based material that continues to breathe after the rug is completed, purifying the surrounding air and absorbing humidity.
www.soejima.com

## Stella rug,
## Michelle Mason

Made from 100 percent undyed merino wool, Michelle Mason's Stella is a contemporary take on traditional lacemaking.
www.michellemason.co.uk

### Broadloom carpet, Angela Adams, Shaw Contract Group

Constructed using a cradle-to-cradle nylon containing 25 percent recycled content, Angela Adams' broadloom carpet tiles (far left) and carpets (left) can be completely recycled at the end of their life.
www.shawcontractgroup.com

### Nature and Nurture carpets, The Alternative Flooring Company

Hand woven on traditional looms, in colours drawn from the natural world, Nature and Nurture is a collection of organic, textured natural wool carpets. The collection has been awarded the International Oeko-Tex Certificate, in recognition of being free of any harmful substances. In these carpets, the woollen thread is woven onto a base of cotton and jute, with a cotton backing secured by a natural latex layer, rather than standard synthetic materials.
www.alternativeflooring.co.uk

## Felt rugs, Felt

Felt's unique rugs are made in fairtrade conditions by the nomadic people of the remote Tien Shan mountains in Kyrgyzstan. Known as shrydaks, these wool rugs have a tough, flattened felt base handsewn with geometric surface patterns in natural undyed or coloured felts. In addition to paying a fair price for the nomad's rugs, Felt also returns an additional 5 percent of the UK selling price to support the wider shrydak-making community in Kyrgyzstan.
www.feltrugs.co.uk

## Papyra rug, Ulf Moritz, Danskina

Hand tufted from 55 percent pure new wool and 45 percent recycled paper, Papyra is a strong and sustainable rug. The paper included in the design is treated with natural wax, which makes the rug resistant to water and dirt.
www.danskina.com

## Carpet tiles, Renewal

Renewal carpet tiles are produced from at least 70 percent recycled materials and are completely recyclable and biodegradable.
www.renewalcarpettiles.com

## Wooden flooring, Dinesen

Made using wood sourced only from sustainable forests, the wide, distinctive planks of a solid Dinesen floor are made to last many lifetimes.
www.dinesen-floors.com

## Natural alpaca carpet, Velieris

Velieris create luxury carpets made from 100 percent sustainable alpaca. The wool is left undyed to highlight the yarn's natural beauty.
www.velieris.com

### Marmoleum floor covering, Forbo

This natural floor covering, which carries the British Allergy Foundation's Seal of Approval, is available in 30 colourways and differently sized panels and squares, allowing you to create your own custom design.
www.forbo-flooring.co.uk

### Marmoleum floor covering, Forbo

A natural flooring made from linseed oil, wood flour, rosin, jute and limestone, Forbo's Marmoleum is a hygienic, antistatic and biodegradable floor covering.
www.forbo-flooring.co.uk

### Touch floor covering, Forbo

Made from natural, raw materials, including linseed oil, wood flour, jute and limestone, Touch is a linoleum-based floor covering range with the tactile quality of cork.
www.forbo-flooring.co.uk

# Products

## Iniko bicycle storage unit, Iniko Design

The Iniko cycle storage unit offers a secure solution to cycle theft and also allows you to store your bike, helmet and other belongings in a weatherproof environment. The product is made using recycled materials and is designed to be easily recycled at the end of its life.
www.inikodesign.com

## Cycloc bicycle storage unit, Andrew Lang

Cycloc is bike storage with a twist, allowing you to store your bike in style. Particularly suited to urban cyclists with small living spaces, Cycloc allows users to simply hang their bike on their wall as you would hang up your jacket. All versions of Cycloc could be considered eco-sensitive as they actively encourage the use of bicycles, however the black version is superior as it is produced from 100 percent recycled post-industrial MDPE waste.
www.andrewlang.co.uk

## Recycle unit, Bisley

Designed for offices, the Bisley recycle unit is made from 40 percent recycled steel and is completely recyclable.
www.bisley.com

### Wedge Racer, Gitta Gschwendtner, Twentytwentyone

Constructed from sustainably sourced wood, Gitta Gschwendtner's Wedge Racer can be enjoyed by children and adults alike, hopefully giving the product a longer lifespan.
www.twentytwentyone.com

### EmPowered Composter, Wiggly Wigglers

Designed to be used indoors, Wiggly Wigglers EmPowered bin composts kitchen waste quickly and discreetly. The bucket, made from recycled plastic, is small enough to fit into a compact space and has an air-tight lid to seal away any smells. The system relies on EmPowered Bokashi Active Bran to speed up the composting process.
www.wigglywigglers.co.uk

### Pet Pod, Vaccari

Inspired by the designer's cat, the Pet Pod is a hand-fashioned dome made out of recycled newspapers and telephone directories for cats and small dogs.
www.vaccari.co.uk

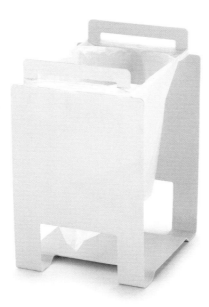

## Ben the Bin, Max McMurdo, Reestore

Made entirely from recycled materials such as plastic drink bottles, Ben is a bin designed to promote household recycling of household waste. The design provides a useful function for the stockpiles of carrier bags many of us have in our homes.
www.reestore.com

## Poubelle dustbin, Paola Navone, Opinion Ciatti

These rubber dustbins are made from recycled tyres and are perfect for use as tidy baskets or recycling bins.
www.opinionciatti.com

## Bin bag, Krejci

Using unconventional materials, Krejci has created a range of recycled handmade designs like the Bin bag. Made from used bicycle inner tubes with a felt lining, it is perfect for tidying or shopping.
www.krejci.nl

### Woodshell Bioplastic Computer, Fujitsu and Monacca

This laptop was shown at the Japan 2008 Design Fair. It is a collaboration between electonics company Fujitsu and Monacca, and its outer is constructed from sustainably sourced steam-bent Japanese cedar. 30 percent of the computer's housing and plastic parts are made from corn-based bioplastics.
www.monacca.net

### One Laptop Per Child, Yves Behar, Fuse Project

One Laptop Per Child, or OLPC, is a non-profit organization committed to bringing technology and education to millions of children in developing countries worldwide. Designed for children, this laptop is a compact, durable product with both a coloured image screen and a high-contrast black-and-white screen for reading text.
www.fuseproject.com

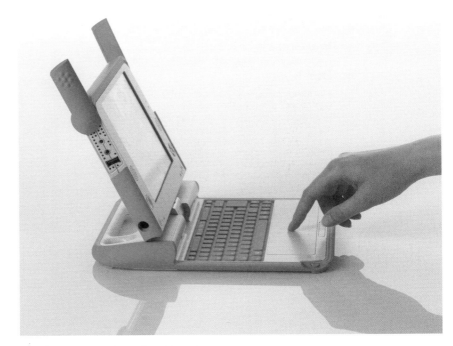

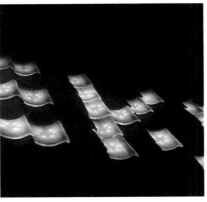

### Light-emitting roof tiles, Lambert Kamps

With these solar powered roof tiles it is possible to apply huge texts, logos and animations onto your roof.
www.lambertkamps.com

### Sandy Eco rechargeable portable phone, Tej and Sach Chauhan, Chauhan Studio

Made from 100 percent recycled plastic, Sandy Eco is a rechargeable portable phone for the home, which features an 'eco' mode to transmit less power when it is not in use. The phone comes in a simple recyclable giftbox, with full instructions printed on recycled paper.
www.tejchauhan.com

### Wattson electricity monitoring device, DIY Kyoto

Wattson is an electricity monitoring device for your home that tells you how much energy your house is consuming at any given time. The device is portable, so can be placed anywhere in your home as it receives the information from a transmitter attached to your electricity meter or fusebox. By monitoring their usage, users often find that they save up to 20 percent on their electricity bill.
www.diykyoto.com

### Tana WaterBar T6 water purifier, New Deal Design

Billions of plastic water bottles end up in landfill every year. By refusing to buy and use plastic bottles and drinking tap water you can greatly reduce the amount of waste you produce.
The Tana WaterBar T6 is a water purifier of the highest standard that can dispense both hot and cold water at precise, specified temperatures. It is made using recycled plastic and all pieces can be easily replaced.
www.newdealdesign.com

## Pure-Malt speakers, Pioneer

Winner of a resource-recycling technology prize, Pure-Malt speakers are made from 50-year-old white oak whisky barrels, said to imbue the speakers with a warm, rich sound.
www.pioneer.co.uk

## Portable DVD player, Philips

Slim, energy-efficient portable DVD player with rechargeable battery, suitable for use anywhere.
www.philips.co.uk

## Dentaku wooden calculator, Monacca

Made from sustainably sourced steam-bent cedar, Monacca's handmade calculators are handmade by skilled craftsmen.
www.monacca.net

## ICF-B01 portable radio, Sony

Turning the handle of this wind-up radio for just one minute is sufficient to power the AM tuner for an hour or to make a three-minute call on your mobile phone if it needs charging. It is also equipped with two different high-intensity LED lights that are handy in the event of a power cut.
www.sony.co.uk

## Ambisound Home Theatre System, Philips

Consuming 50 percent less energy than its closest competitor, Philips Ambisound Home Theatre System provides a full surround home entertainment experience.
www.philips.co.uk

### Eco Kettle, Ecoutlet

The Energy Savings Trust recently reported that 67 percent of UK householders habitually boil more water than is needed in the kettle. The Eco Kettle seeks to solve this problem by allowing the user to fill the kettle to its maximum; then by pressing the measuring button, you allow any quantity – from a single cupful to full capacity – to be released into the separate chamber for boiling.
www.ecoutlet.co.uk

### Solio Charger, Solio

A solar-powered universal charger compatible with almost all mobile phones, MP3 players, PDAs and handheld games, the Solio Charger simplifies your life and saves energy.
www.solio.com

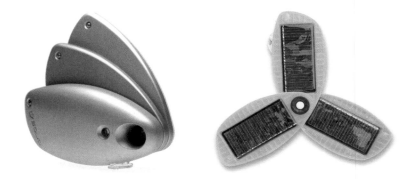

### Walkman® S Series, Sony

Sony's Walkman® S Series is designed to operate with maximum efficiency using 75 percent less energy than the previous models.
www.sony.co.uk

### Jar Tops, Jorre van Ast, RVKB

RVKB's polypropylene Jar Tops transform generic used jam jars into useful kitchenware, prolonging their useful life. The family includes a sugar pot, milk can, spice cellar, chocolate sprinkler, general storage container, oil and vinegar set, a mug and a water jug.
www.jorrevanast.com

## EcoClassic 50 energy-saving lamp, Philips

The Philips EcoClassic 50 is the first ever energy-saving lamp. It allows you to save energy without compromising the visual effect of your lighting installation. Whether at an intimate dining table setting or in a hotel lobby, the lamp creates an authentic and luxurious impression.
www.philips.co.uk

## Gaya wall-mounted fireplace, Roderick Vos, Safretti

A wall-mounted aluminium fireplace designed by Roderick Vos for Safretti, Gaya burns bio-ethanol, an 'alcohol' residue derived from the skin of potatoes. As the bio-ethanol evaporates, the simple, torch-like flame is illuminated. A clean design, Gaya is safe, recyclable, sustainable, and also reduces fuel usage.
www.safretti.com

## Oeko washer and dryer, Electrolux

Electrolux's washer and dryer machines feature a low-energy eco setting.
www.electrolux.com

## Omop disposable mop, Karim Rashid, Method

The Omop is designed to combine the best of disposable mopping systems with eco-sensitive design features. Excellent at cleaning all types of floor, Omop includes compostable sweeper cloths that can simply be added to your compost heap and returned to the Earth once you have finished with them.
www.methodhome.com

## Ultra Silencer cylinder cleaner, Electrolux

Designed to be four times quieter than an average vacuum cleaner, Electrolux's Ultra Silencer cylinder has a low-energy eco setting fitted as standard.
www.electrolux.com

## Standby switch and extension, &made

Focusing on raising awareness of the consumption of electricity through standby appliances and adaptors, &made's Standby makes itself highly visible and available to unplug or switch off rather than hiding itself behind furniture and in corners. www.and-made.com

## Mobile Plastic, Smile Plastics

Commingled recycled plastics feature flow and patterning streaks, which allude to the products' previous uses. Smile Plastics' Mobile Plastic is made of recycled mobile phone fascias and is available in a variety of widths and thicknesses. www.smile-plastics.co.uk

## Oxygen fire, EcoSmart

EcoSmart fires are flueless and do not require any installation or utility connection for fuel supply. Fuelled by a renewable modern energy (denatured ethanol), it burns clean and is virtually maintenance free. www.ecosmartfire.com

## Balanced flue fire, Platonic Fireplaces

An energy-efficient alternative to a standard gas fire, a balanced flue fire operates through the use of an enclosed combustion chamber. Combustion air is drawn into the chamber through a concentric flue system that combines inlet and outlet air movement and works on natural draught. The fireplaces are glass fronted, and save up to 75 percent in gas consumption. www.platonicfireplaces.co.uk

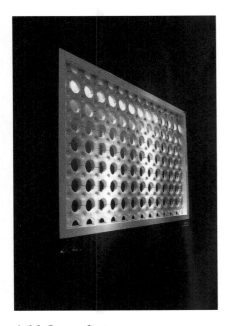

## Add-On radiator,
## Satyendra Pakhalé,
## Tubes Radiatori

Radiators are traditionally technical-looking items; however Pakhale's Add-On radiator covers a much larger surface and could be integrated into an architectural setting – just like a room divider or a window. It uses much less power than a conventional radiator to heat a much larger space. and is more successful at radiating heat throughout a room.
www.tubesradiatori.com

## Fret flat
## speaker panel,
## Studiomold

Fret is a flat speaker panel with laser-cut fretwork. Made from recycled cardboard and recyclable plastic, the speaker is compatible with all MP3 players and personal stereos.
www.studiomold.co.uk

## Wind fan,
## Jasper Startup,
## Gervasoni

Using sustainably sourced woven rattan, Jasper Startup's fan for Gervasoni redefines the nature of home and office cooling systems.
www.gervasoni1882.it

### Shopping bag, Re-found Objects

Recycled cement sacks from India provide the raw materials for Re-found Objects' colourful and versatile shopping bag.
www.re-foundobjects.com

### Kaku bag, Takumi Shimamura, Monacca

Monacca's Kaku bag is constructed from sustainably sourced steam-bent Japanese cedar.
www.monacca.net

### Plastic basket, Hen & Hammock

Hen & Hammock's colourful range of baskets, made from recycled plastic packaging tape, are suitable for laundry or shopping.
www.henandhammock.co.uk

## Just Beg Bag,
## Naulila Luis, Sushi

The Just Beg Bag by Naulila Luis makes clever use of worn out felt-tip marker pens. This fun and colourful design is produced at the Drug-free Unit of the Tires Detention Facility in Lisbon, Portugal.
www.sushidesign.com.pt

## Organic Cotton Bag,
## Hen & Hammock

Made from organic cotton string, this bag fits neatly into a pocket, reducing the need to use plastic bags when out shopping. The bag is fairtrade-assured and produced in India.
www.henandhammock.co.uk

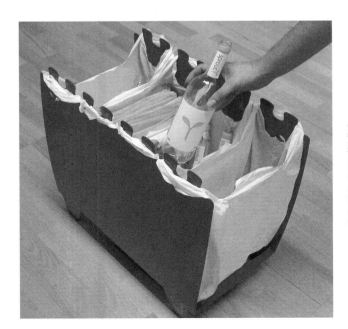

## Binvention recycling bin,
## Sprout Design

Ideal for anyone with a hoard of used plastic carrier bags, Binvention transforms them into simple compartments for sorting cans, paper, bottles and plastic, making for a simple and effective recycling system.
www.sproutdesign.co.uk

# Outdoors

### Broadleaf Chair,
### Terence Conran, Benchmark

Inspired by the beauty of spring and the perfection of newly formed leaves, Terence Conran's Broadleaf Chair features crisp, clean lines and a comfortably curved seat, all made from FSC authenticated oak with a natural, non-toxic oiled finish.
www.benchmark-furniture.com

### Garden seat,
### Nick Barberton

Nick Barberton's stylish garden seat is constructed from sustainably sourced local oak.
www.nickbarberton.co.uk

### Food Altar table
### and benches,
### Andy Wood

Andy Wood chooses reclaimed timbers for his beautifully crafted work, reducing the demand on the Earth's forests. The wood used in Food Altar is centuries old and has been weathered by the elements, imbuing the timber with immense natural beauty.
www.andywood.eu

### Garden furniture range,
### Farley Spencer Fung,
### Daylesford Organic

Farley is a range of teal oak furniture that will age gracefully, bleaching to a beautiful silver-grey colour with time and weather, to harmonize with the garden surroundings. All the timber has FSC and PEFC certification – the twin gold standards of environmental sensitivity.
www.daylesfordorganic.com

### Blooming Bench,
### Tom Hatfield, Benchmark

This beautiful and innovative self-watering garden bench is perfect for year-round use. The pot can easily be filled with different vegetables, flowers or herbs depending on the season. The seat and frame are constructed from FSC authenticated oak with a natural, non-toxic oiled finish, while the pot is made from frost-resistant terracotta.
benchmark-furniture.com

### Jaca table,
### Carlos Motta

Brazilian designer Carlos Motta began creating furniture from driftwood washed ashore in São Paolo. He is now renowned for his environmentally sustainable designs, which are all created from recycled or reused wood. The Jaca table is made from urucurana, a tropical hardwood.
www.carlosmotta.com.br

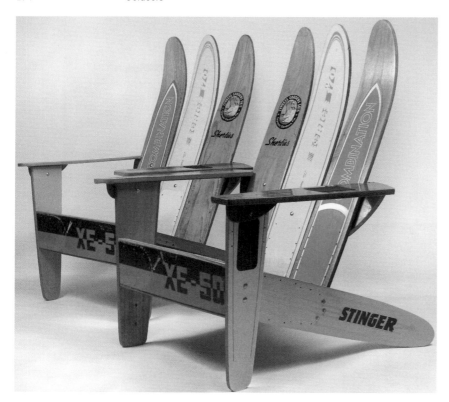

## Hydrorondacks outdoor chair, Chase DeForest

By recycling vintage water skis into the traditional Adirondack chair form, Chase DeForest have created Hydrorondacks, an ironic outdoor chair that is water and weather resistant due to the material's previous treatment.
www.chasedeforest.com

## Terra! armchair, Nucleo

Terra! is not a finished product, it is an idea. Nucleo provide the cardboard frame and then you find the main ingredient, the soil! By burying the cardboard frame in turf, the armchair is born in your garden and becomes part of your landscape. Eventually the frame decomposes, yet the chair remains.
www.nucleo.to

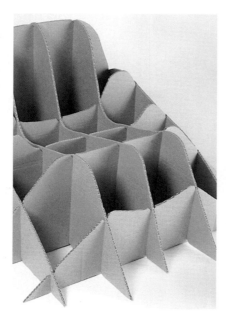

### Once a Door chair,
### Claire Heather Danthois

Claire Heather Danthois creates sculptural and functional furniture using recycled timber, in this case an old door. The curve of the chair is created using a steel cable, eliminating the use of glue or toxins.
www.coroflot.com

### Hosepipe Chair,
### Sander Bokkinga

Amazingly, Sander Bokkinga's chair, made by coiling and knotting old hosepipes, is still able to function as a hosepipe with the water running straight through the design.
www.sanderbokkinga.nl

### Relax furniture set,
### Ineke Hans

Made from recycled plastic, Ineke Hans' Relax furniture set is wind, water, salt, and UV resistant, making it perfect for use inside or outdoors.
www.inekehans.com

### Classic Bench,
### Hen & Hammock

With its curved back and contoured seat, this reclaimed teak bench is both beautiful and comfortable. Oiled with a natural, non-toxic finish, the wood will age elegantly over the years to a soft silver-grey. Each piece of teak is carefully salvaged, from sources independently audited by both the FSC and SmartWood®.
www.henandhammock.co.uk

## Chaise Longue No.4, Tom Raffield

Designer Tom Raffield specializes in making pioneering, ecologically sound furniture and lighting. This chair is his signature piece, and is as elegant as it is functional. Constructed from sustainably sourced solid British oak, the chair demonstrates how wood can be used to make complex yet beautiful three-dimensional forms. www.tomraffield.com

## Pigalle chair, Kenneth Cobonpue

Grounded in minimalism but with a sensuous outline of curves, the Pigalle chair is constructed from abaca fibres, which are hand processed, cleaned of pulps and accumulated into vines and ropes. These are tied onto a recycled and hand sculpted frame of light steel. www.kennethcobonpue.com

## Lolah armchair, Kenneth Cobonpue

Lolah is a strong yet light armchair, constructed from rattan strips bound onto a rattan frame using an innovative technique similar to ancient boatbuilding. The rattan is sourced from the woodlands of Mindanao, an island in the Philippines that is rich in natural resources. The rattan pole is cut into strips and individually bent by steam in a process that costs a fraction of the time and energy required to bend wood. www.kennethcobonpue.com

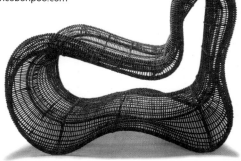

## Nananu chair, David Trubridge

This beautiful sculptural form is an occasional chair made with steam-bent untreated wood. www.davidtrubridge.com

## Hanging chair, Raw Studio

Cut concentrically from the same sheet of FSC approved wood, this hanging chair creates no waste in its production. There are no fixings or extra glues used either, the design relying simply on a rope and gravity. Each piece of furniture is made locally, with chairs for the UK created in Kent, while Sydney is the base for the Australian market. This process saves shipping and the process could be developed for any market.
www.rawstudio.co.uk

## Rolling Summer House, Charlie Whinney

Rolling Summer House is an extraordinary spherical structure, which is large enough to relax inside yet light enough for an adult to roll around a garden in. Constructed from sustainably sourced steam-bent timber, the frame is also strong enough to be used as a climbing frame for children and can be safely anchored to the ground.
www.charliewhinney.com

## Once a Gate seat, Claire Heather Danthois

This seat, made from an old gate, is also left free from paint or unnecessary finishes, avoiding a possible source of pollution.
www.corofiot.com

## Rainbow Hammock, Amazonas, Hen & Hammock

The Brazilian hammock-making industry is threatened by increasing volumes of cheap foam mattresses from the Far East. Fighting this influx of environmentally unfriendly materials, this hammock is made from strong, colourful cotton to the highest standards by Amazonas, a fairtrade organization in Ceará, one of the poorest regions of Brazil.
www.henand hammock.co.uk

## Ting's Sling hammock, Inghua Ting, TING

Ting's Sling is hand woven using reclaimed seatbelt fabric in a choice of bright shades including lime green, orange, silver, camel or chocolate.
www.tinglondon.com

## Bench, Barry Feldman, Woodworksdesigns

Barry Feldman creates unique furniture using sustainably sourced timbers.
www.woodworksdesigns.co.uk

### Deckchair,
### Hen & Hammock

The perfect way to enjoy a summer's day, this folding deckchair, handmade from sustainable beech, is built to last.
www.henandhammock.co.uk

### Reminiscence Bench,
### Ineke Hans/Arnhem

Made out of FSC certified wood, the Reminiscence Bench is produced in an arrangement with Staatsbosbeheer (The Royal Dutch Forest Organization) whereby donors to the organization can have a bench with the inscription of their choice placed in one of the hundreds of Staatsbosbeheer forests. Planted with a sapling through a hole in the extended seat, the tree eventually grows to form a kind of parasol, offering shade to the sitter.
www.inekehans.com

### Somewhere Over
### the Rainbow swing,
### Marnie Moyle

Marnie Moyle carves decorative words into the surfaces of her sustainably sourced, untreated oak furniture. The words and phrases tell a story – enjoying provenance, she tells of where the trees once stood, who commissioned the work, when it was made and even why.
www.marniemoyle.co.uk

## Gulliver's Chair, Julienne Dolphin-Wilding

Julienne Dolphin-Wilding's Gulliver's Chair is made from carved telegraph poles, with nautical rope upholstery.
www.dolphinwilding.com

## Love Seat, Julienne Dolphin-Wilding

Salvaged English yew is used to create Julienne Dolphin-Wilding's Love Seat. As the material is found and reused, each piece is unique. The inherent qualities and features of the found materials inspire the themes in her work.
www.dolphinwilding.com

## Bench, Marnie Moyle

Marnie Moyle uses sustainably sourced unseasoned oak for its longevity, but also because the nature of green (unseasoned) timber is that it will move, shrink and sometimes twist, adding to the uniqueness of her work.
www.marniemoyle.co.uk

### Twiggy Bench, Doug Wightman

All the wood in the Twiggy Bench comes from nearby fallen trees or timber cut from Doug Wightman's own garden.
dwightman@doctors.org.uk

### Parati chaise longue, Carlos Motta

All of Carlos Motta's products are created from locally sourced, reused and recycled materials. The Parati chaise longue is designed for lazing on the beach and is made from reused peroba rosa, a native Brazilian tree that is also used in beekeeping equipment.
www.carlosmotta.com.br

### Twiggy Chair, Doug Wightman

Like the Twiggy Bench, the Twiggy Chair is entirely constructed from locally sourced or fallen timber.
dwightman@doctors.org.uk

### Bench,
### Baccarne Design

This outdoor bench is completely made of recycled plastics, gathered from sheets of household and commercial waste. Ultra durable, with high longevity, it needs zero maintenance and is incredibly difficult for vandals to destroy.
www.baccarne.be

### Plants Table,
### Marnie Moyle

Coming from a precious cabinet-making background, Marnie Moyle has no fear of the sustainably sourced, untreated oak that she uses for her outdoor furniture range. Initially encouraging people to scratch words into her work, she has now refined her decorative style into her distinctive carving, which brings a familial sense of belonging to her work.
www.marniemoyle.co.uk

### Go Club Chair,
### Greg Benson, Dave Benson
### and Tony Ciardelli,
### Loll Designs

Inspired by traditional chairs found in gentlemen's clubs, the Go Club Chair is updated for the outdoors by being made out of 100 percent post-consumer recycled plastic.
www.lolldesigns.com

### Eureka hanging chair, Giovanni Travasa, Vittorio Bonacina

Sustainable rattan is used to produce the elegant curves of Vittorio Bonacina's classic Eureka hanging chair.
www.bonacinavittorio.it

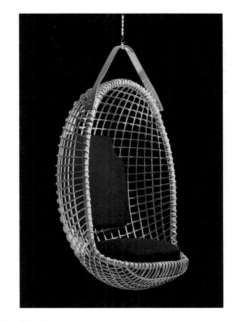

### Ecal stools, Nicolas le Moigne, Eternit

Scraps of Eternit (a lightweight, cost-effective building material) are pushed into a mould and pressed to form the mushroom-shaped stool. As a result of the technique, each stool is slightly different.
www.nicolaslemoigne.com
www.eternit.at

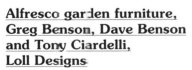

### Alfresco garden furniture, Greg Benson, Dave Benson and Tony Ciardelli, Loll Designs

Loll Designs' furniture is constructed out of 100 percent post-consumer recycled plastic (mostly from milk bottles). The material requires no maintenance and is completely weatherproof and eventually recyclable.
www.lolldesigns.com

## TransPlastic chair, Fernando and Humberto Campana, Estúdio Campana

Part of the Campana brothers' 'TransPlastic' collection, the chair consists of reused plastic waste set within woven apuí, a natural Brazilian fibre. Extraction of this fibre helps preserve and control the biodiversity of the forests, as apuí suffocates and kills the trees on which it grows. The fibres are removed manually, without any tools or processes that may harm the trees.
www.estudiocampana.com

## +13 chair/container, Fabio Novembre, Frezza

Designed from recycled polyethylene, +13 has a double function: it is a chair and a container for medium-sized trees.
www.frezza.com

## Café chair, Fernando and Humberto Campana, Estúdio Campana

Taking ordinary plastic chairs as a starting point, Fernando and Humberto Campana have added natural apuí fibre extensions to alter the chair's original form.
www.estudiocamp ana.com

## Ruth Rocker,
## David Trubridge, Cappellini

Constructed using either sustainable outdoor plywood or oiled sustainable New Zealand red beech, Ruth by David Trubridge is a simple and elegant outdoor rocking chair.
www.cappellini.it

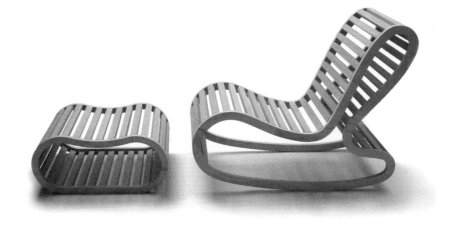

## Ebb bench,
## Matthias Studio

Steam-bent from small strips of wood that would normally be classified as waste, the Ebb bench is designed to resemble plastic forms using natural, sustainable materials. The oak comes from the Timber Growers' Alliance, in Wisconsin, who cut down one tree per acre per year. The trees are dried in a solar kiln, resulting in the perfect wood for steam bending.
www.matthias-studio.com

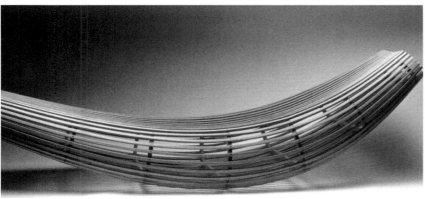

## Body Raft chaise longue,
## David Trubridge, Cappellini

Inspired by the designer's boat-building experience, Body Raft is designed as a rocking chaise longue for either indoor or outdoor use. A timeless yet contemporary design, the sustainable ash and hoop plywood structure contains universal nautical forms from throughout history and is suspended in a hammock, yet supported by a rigid structure.
www.cappellini.it

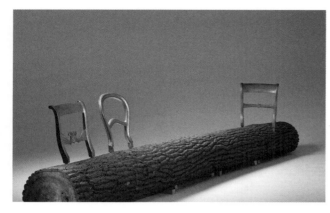

## Treetrunk bench, Jurgen Bay, Droog

Jurgen Bay uses sustainably sourced trees as giant benches. Bronze casts of existing chair backs are fixed into the trunk, transforming the bench into a piece of luxury furniture. This cross-breeding results in a striking interaction between culture and nature.
www.droog.com

## Milking Stool, Helena Bancroft

Without disguising the product's original form, Helena Bancroft has taken a traditional bucket and transformed it into a versatile product with a detachable lid that can be used as a bucket, as a stool or for storage. The new product is a respectful tribute to the old, which highlights the issue of waste in our disposable society.
miss-helena@hotmail.co.uk

## Extrusion chair, Jurgen Bay, Droog

Jurgen Bay compresses garden waste – the hay of the summer, the prunings and leaves of the autumn – into temporary outdoor furniture. Extrusion containers press the garden waste into endless benches, which can be shortened to any length. It is then up to nature to decide when to take them back.
www.droog.com

## Hemisphere chair,
## Richard Frinier, Dedon

Dedon furniture is crafted in a fairtrade environment on the Philippine island of Cebu, using the experience of local weavers. The company's guiding principle is: only a happy employee can invent a comfortable chair.
www.dedon.de

## Leaf chair,
## Richard Frinier,
## Dedon

Each piece of Dedon furniture embodies a combination of modern technology and centuries-old craftsmanship. All pieces are elaborately hand-woven from the weather-resistant Dedon fibre, which is washable, UV-resistant and biodegradable.
www.dedon.de

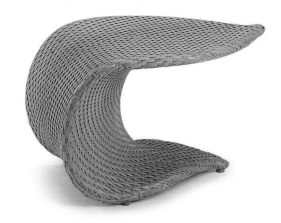

## Orbit loveseat,
## Richard Frinier, Dedon

Orbit by Richard Frinier is a futuristic loveseat, which is crafted in a fairtrade environment on the Philippine island of Cebu.
www.dedon.de

### Transrock chair, Fernando and Humberto Campana, Estúdio Campana

The Transrock chair consists of a plastic chair set within woven apuí.
www.estudiocampana.com

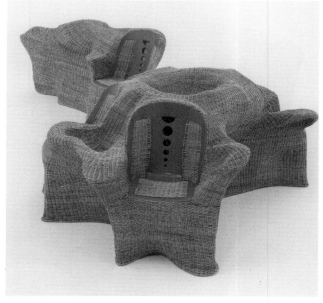

### Kingston furniture, Cane-line

All Cane-line products are hand-wickered with hularo fibres, which are toxin-free, biodegradable and recyclable. The entire collection is incredibly strong, and is far more tolerant to pouring rain and beating sun than traditional cane furniture. The collection is also UV, colour, water and frost resistant and requires no maintenance whatsoever.
www.cane-line.com

### Aluminium Chair, Rob van Acker

This folding chair is formed from the weather-beaten aluminium panels of old Land Rovers in Zambia. Rob van Acker elegantly recycles the material, welding it into a new shape that can continue to be used for decades.
www.robvanacker.com

### Hose Chair, Chase DeForest

By recontextualizing garden hose, Chase DeForest illustrate a creative way to reuse surplus garden and household products.
www.chasedeforest.com

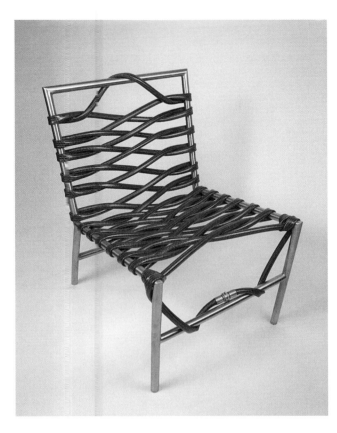

### taTu modular pieces, Stephen Burks, Artecnica

In Zimbabwe's Shona dialect, tatu means 'three', and here refers to the three-fold modularity of each piece. The coffee table converts into a tray, bowl and basket; the side table becomes a tray, bowl and rubbish bin; and the stackable one-piece stool provides seating. A weatherproof polished powder coating makes taTu ideal for both indoor and outdoor spaces.
www.artecnicainc.com

### Sky light, Alfredo Häberli, Luceplan

An outdoor light designed for energy saving lamps, Sky is available in versions with LED with photovoltaic cells and rechargeable batteries, wire-free, or with high-efficiency LED with electronic power supply.
www.luceplan.com

## Let's Grow Some Balls garden/garden chair, Krejci

Both a garden and a garden chair at the same time, Let's Grow Some Balls features a cavity for soil so you can grow your own fruit, flowers or vegetables. Made out of recycled plastic, the chair is also biodegradable.
www.krejci.nl

## Tiles flowerpots, Nicolas le Moigne, Eternit

Nicolas le Moigne uses waste scraps of Eternit, a material made from sheets of cement and paper fibres, to create tiled flowerpots.
www.nicolaslemoigne.com
www.eternit.at

## Form, Roberta Amurri, Metacarta

Using recycled paper, Roberta Amurri creates products as light as paper and as hardy as rock. This is accomplished by using a core of existing secondhand structures, which are then covered with a humid paste of recycled paper. The resulting objects are extra-light, in spite of their monolithic appearance, and as solid, durable and practical as they look.
www.metacarta.it.

## WoodStock log transporter and stacking facility, Dirk Wynants, Extremis

WoodStock was developed with intelligent use of materials. Extremis' goal is to reduce waste materials and create products with respect for nature. In this case, the chariot is made out of the leftover material from the rack.
www.extremis.be

### Leaf and Tree garden tools, Takumi Shimamura, Comore

With elegant simple lines that echo those of nature, Comore's Leaf and Tree gardening trowel and hoe are made from sustainable bamboo. www.comore-ohl.jp

### Mizusashi watering can, Takumi Shimamura, Comore

A simple minimalist watering can, Mizusashi is the size of a milk carton and is constructed from sustainable bamboo. www.comore-ohl.jp

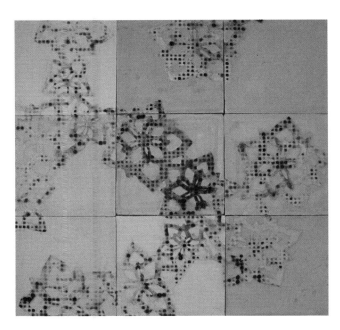

### Come Rain or Shine wallcovering, Heather Smith

Come Rain or Shine works in conjunction with the natural elements – allowing nature itself to bring pattern and decoration to different surfaces. The tiled walls are a combination of laser-cut felt inlaid in plaster. Suitable for outdoor wall panels, the felt will potentially act as a platform for organic matter to grow on. www.heathersmithcollection.com

## Forget Me Knot and Grow plant labels, Blue Marmalade

'The rest of your garden looks beautiful, so why shouldn't your plant labels?' asks Blue Marmalade with its recycled and reusable Forget Me Knot and Grow label kits. Each kit features ten reusable plant labels made from recycled polypropylene, and a Chinagraph pencil. The Forget Me Knot labels, with their floral shape are intended for flower gardens, while the carrot-shaped Grow labels are designed for vegetable gardens. The pencil is waterproof so won't wash off in the rain yet the writing can be wiped off and the label reused.
www.bluemarmalade.co.uk

## Paper Potter pot-maker, Hen & Hammock

Winner of the Green Apple Environment Award, the Paper Potter, made from FSC certified oak, offers an easy way to make biodegradable pots from old newspapers.
www.henandhammock.co.uk

## Watering can, Nicolas le Moigne, Viceversa

Nicolas le Moigne's spout is an easy way to transform used plastic bottles into a watering can. The screw-on spout fits a variety of plastic or glass bottles and is available in a range of five colours.
www.nicolaslemoigne.com
www.viceversa.it

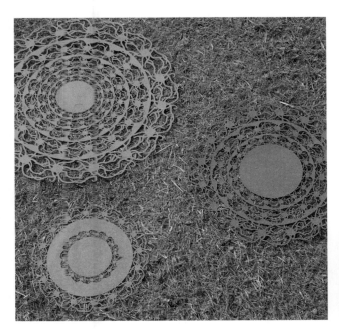

## Garden Doilies, Charlotte Miller

Cut from sailmakers' waste materials, Garden Doilies are a sustainable product inspired by nature and the natural environment. The sails are laser cut, with marine-inspired imagery, which links the material's previous use to its current one.

## Recycled bobbin and string, Hen & Hammock

A piece of British industrial history, Hen & Hammock's bobbins have been salvaged from Lancashire cotton mills and recycled with orange jute twine. Bobbin colours vary, but all are beautifully worn. Lancashire cotton mills used bobbins from the mechanization of weaving and spinning from the mid-nineteenth century onwards, and many had coloured ends to distinguish them. These coloured ends now have a wonderful worn patina.
www.henandhammock.co.uk

## Plant labels, Hen & Hammock

Individually made from sustainable English oak, these labels will last for years, weathering to a rich grey-brown. Writing can be erased with a rubber or with fine sandpaper, allowing the labels to be used again and again.
www.henandhammock.co.uk

## City Vegetable Garden allotment structure, Eco Outlet

The City Vegetable Garden provides a space dedicated to growing edible plants in an urban environment and is perfect for indoor and outdoor growing in a small kitchen or balcony. Designed with sustainability in mind, the allotment structure is made of anodized aluminium, is light, unbreakable and 100 percent recyclable. The structure also has a drainage system that prevents excessive watering.
www.ecoutlet.co.uk

## Recycled plant pot holder, Kim Jenkins, Hen & Hammock

Thousands of sacks are used every day to transport fruit and vegetables to London markets. These useful sacks are clean, colourful and strong, but typically go into landfill straight afterwards. Fortunately, Kim Jenkins collects them and transforms them into unique plant pot holders.
www.henandhammock.co.uk

## Recycled glass cloche, Hen & Hammock

Made from recycled glass, this Victorian-style glass cloche offers a traditional way to protect tender plants from frost, insects, birds and strong winds. The curved shape allows the surface of the cloche always to be perpendicular to the direction of the sun, thereby achieving minimum refraction and maximum penetration of light for an optimum growing environment.
www.henandhammock.co.uk

## Recycled tyre trug, Hen & Hammock

Modelled on reed tubs used by early archaeologists, this recycled tyre trug is cut and hand sewn from a used tyre. The rubber is tough, malleable and surprisingly light, making it ideal for use in the home or garden.
www.henandhammock.co.uk

## Planted Settle with Moss Seat, Julienne Dolphin-Wilding

Made using found and recycled materials, Julienne Dolphin-Wilding's Planted Settle has a moss seat, which lifts up to allow for garden storage.
dolphin-wilding.com

## Modular growhouse, Daniel Schippervouwkas

Ideal for gardening in small spaces such as balconies, roof terraces or town gardens, Daniel Schippervouwkas' innovative, lightweight, flexible modular greenhouse has a frameless construction made of recyclable plastic, which can be folded flat or expanded when required. The result is a beautiful and practical growhouse.
www.danielschipper.nl

## Billbirdhouse, Antoinet Deurloo and Michael Bom, Atelier Bom Design

Nesting boxes range from the clean and modern to the purely practical, but, whatever the design, they are a great way to encourage birds into urban environments. This simply constructed birdhouse is made from old billboards and found hardware, making each box unique.
www.bomdesign.nl

## Shop Sign Bird Houses, Peter Marigold

Made from salvaged shop signs and crate material, Peter Marigold's irregular shaped bird houses use waste material to provide a nesting place for wildlife.
www.petermarigold.com

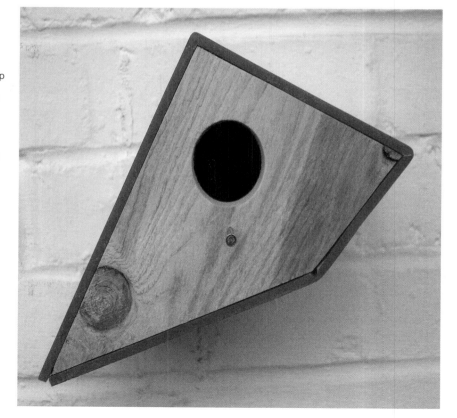

### Penguin, Trend Group

Made using 80 percent post-consumer recycled glass, this happy penguin forms part of Trend Group's Animal Collection of garden decorations. www.trend-vi.com

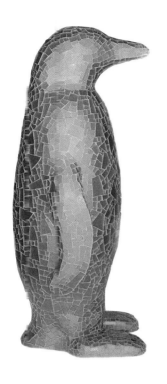

### Clog Box, Wiggly Wigglers

Handmade by a Dutch clog-maker, the Clog Box is shaped from the toe section of an oversized clog. It makes a lovely, curvy focal point for any natural garden and the hole size is perfect for blue tits and other garden birds. www.wigglywigglers.co.uk

### A Bird's Palace, Doreen Westphal, KREJCI

Designed by Amsterdam-based designer Doreen Westphal, the bird's house is made by a small ceramic family business in Meissen, Germany. www.krejci.nl

### Beehive Composter, Wiggly Wigglers

The aim of Wiggly Wigglers is to sell objects that help Planet Earth get on with its job. The Beehive Composter can be nestled in among the vegetable patch or flower garden, or anywhere waste can be added conveniently. Compost will then be ready to use where you want it.
www.wigglywigglers.co.uk

### Birdhouse Schwegler, Wiggly Wigglers

Made from woodcrete, a material that feels and looks a little like concrete but is actually made from 75 percent wood, the Schwegler birdhouse is endorsed by a wide range of bird conservation groups. This is because woodcrete is fully breathable as well as being a great insulator, thus keeping the birdhouses' inhabitants warm.
www.wigglywigglers.co.uk

### Maisonette nesting box, Eva Guillet and Aruna Ratnayake, Studio Lo

This fuzzy nesting box is made using water-jet cut natural grey felt. The box is flat-packed for easy assembly at home, and the roof can be opened to clean out each autumn. At the end of its life, the box will simply decompose.
studio.lo.neuf.fr

### Terracotta Birdball, Gavin Christman and Kate Knapp, Hen & Hammock

The Terracotta Birdball is a great example of innovative design combined with a traditional manufacturing process. The hole is large enough to allow easy access for blue tits, coal tits and marsh tits, but small enough to keep out predators. Only natural ingredients are used, so when the Birdball finally reaches the end of its life, its disposal does not present an eco-hazard.
www.henandhammock.co.uk

### Sedum-roofed birdhouse, Hen & Hammock

Living roofs absorb carbon dioxide and attract butterflies, bees and ladybirds. If you're not ready to convert your entire roof, why not try a sedum-roofed birdhouse? Made using traditional woodworking skills and locally sourced FSC approved timber, these boxes make fine homes for birds.
www.henandhammock.co.uk

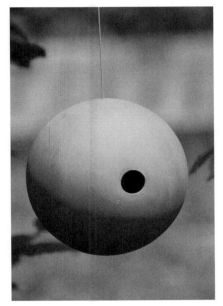

### 'Cabane des Oiseaux' bird feeder, Atelier Oi

Atelier Oi's 'Cabane des Oiseaux' (bird hut) house-shaped feeder is designed for small garden birds to nest in. As the birds peck happily away at the seeds, the house will slowly disappear, leaving no trace or debris behind.
www.atelier-oi.ch

### Solar LED house number, Ecoutlet

These solar LED house numbers are laser-cut from anodized aluminium and absorb light during the day, powering a solar cell and two high bright LEDs that display the house number at night and create a 3D effect.
www.ecoutlet.co.uk

### Ecoblock outdoor torch, Hen & Hammock

Made from environmentally friendly pine, the Ecoblock is a natural outdoor torch, which burns down completely after 50 to 60 minutes. The pine is sourced from sustainable plantations used for furniture manufacture. The forests are cleared of dead wood before the harvest, then this dead wood is kiln-dried and cut into shape to form the Ecoblock.
www.henand hammock.co.uk

### Windmills, Julienne Dolphin-Wilding

Julienne Dolphin-Wilding's decorative Windmills are made using recycled brass and copper.
www.dolphinwilding.com

### Reused coffee sacks, Hen & Hammock

Used to bring green coffee beans to the UK from countries like Columbia, Ethiopia and India, sacks woven of jute, hemp or flax are 100 percent natural and biodegradable and can easily be reused in the garden.
www.henand hammock.co.uk

## Lumi illuminated rainwater storage, Fulltank

Designed for those who are proud of their commitment to saving rainwater, Lumi can potentially cut household water consumption by 20 percent, while also acting as a modern architectural design and lighting feature. It is designed for minimum wastage of materials and uses only fully recyclable materials. The tank is also lit with low-energy consumption LEDs that give the clean, contemporary lines a soft, stylish glow at night. www.fulltank.com.au

## Garden lanterns, Hen & Hammock

Made from recycled glass wrapped in a wire frame, these garden lanterns are made in Vietnam, under fairtrade conditions. www.henandhammock.co.uk

# Kids

### Eco Cradle, Ecoutlet

The Eco Cradle is a stylish, innovative product made entirely of cardboard that meets the changing needs of a young baby in a sustainable fashion. Designed for the first few months in the home, the cradle is made from more than 60 percent recycled material and is safe, light and easily to put up and take down, The structure is also protected by an environmentally friendly, non-toxic fire retardant. www.ecoutlet.co.uk

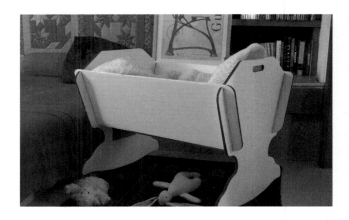

### Spring Celebration Crib, Lilipad Studios

Constructed from FSC certified hardwood and painted with zero-VOC paints, Lilipad Studio's crib is an ecologically sensitive celebration of spring. www.lilipadstudioshop.com

### loLine Changing Trunk, Michaele Simmering and Johannes Pauwen, Kalon Studios

With its clean, functional simplicity, the loLine Changing Trunk is designed to fit anywhere around the home. Made from sustainably sourced bamboo plywood and non-toxic glue, the trunk is finished with a 100 percent natural non-toxic finish, and is manufactured locally. www.kalonstudios.com

### The Animals of Whittling Wood coat hook, Carl Clerkin, Twentytwentyone

Crafted from sustainable wood, Carl Clerkin's Animals of Whittling Wood aims to strengthen the attachment between people and their belongings. By creating characters within objects, he hopes to slow down landfill and encourage people to foster stronger relations with their surroundings.
www.twentytwentyone.com

### Sparrow crib or toddler bed, Oeuf

Made of wood from a sustainable birch forest, which is manufactured under strict environmental guidelines, the Sparrow crib can be easily converted to form a toddler bed, prolonging its lifespan.
www.oeufnyc.com

### Bugs and Leaves bed linen, Luma

Made in a sumptuous 200 thread-count organic cotton percale, Luma's children's bed linen shares the same excellent quality and eco credentials as their adult ranges.
www.lumadirect.com

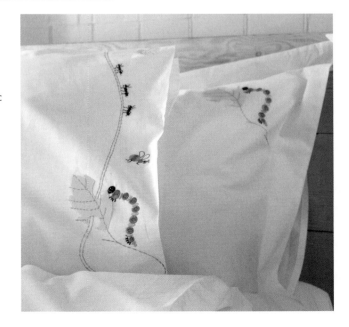

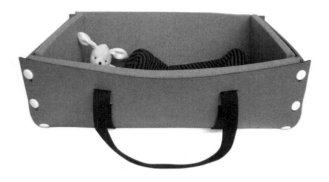

### 'And my baby goes so well with it!' Moses basket, Britta Teleman

'And my baby goes so well with it!' is a lightweight Moses basket that can be moved easily between rooms and disassembled for transport, or stored away. All the materials used, including cork, felt and cotton, are renewable, recycled or organic; and, as the crib comes flat-packed, to be assembled by the user, energy used in transportation is minimized.
www.objecthood.se

### Le Petit Voyage crib, Kenneth Cobonpue

This cosy cocoon is made of abaca vine and buri, some of the finest natural fibres in the world. Buri is one of the six species of palms that are also referred to as fan palms, while abaca is extracted from the abaca plant or Manila hemp. Recycled metal provides the frame for this crib, and no toxins or artificial finishes are applied to the material at all.
www.kennethcobonpue.com

### Aalto Cot, George Gold Furniture Design

Made from leftovers and off-cuts from other projects, George Gold's Aalto Cot is a pleasing patchwork of timber. The cot, made to order, can later be converted into a bed, giving the product a much longer useful life.
www.georgegoldfurnituredesign.co.uk

## Toddler Birch Bed, Oeuf

Offering an easy transition from crib to bed, Oeuf's Toddler Birch Bed is equipped with safety rails that don't hinder a child's ability to climb in and out. The bed is constructed from solid birch and non-toxic white lacquer.
www.oeufnyc.com

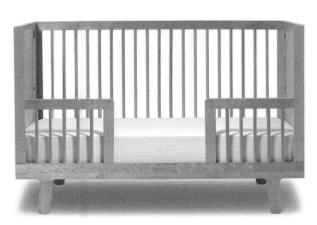

## loLine Crib, Michaele Simmering and Johannes Pauwen, Kalon Studios

Built from sustainable materials, the loLine crib promises elegance, comfort and practicality in one design. It is manufactured from sustainable bamboo using CNC Milling, a method that offers 95 percent material efficiency. When it's time, the crib also changes into a toddler bed, prolonging the product's life.
www.kalonstudios.com

### Happy Stripe printed fabric, Nya Nordiska

A printed fabric with multi-coloured, broad stripes, Happy Stripe is awarded the Oeko-Tex Standard 100, which guarantees it is an untreated fabric without any chemical finishing and no allergic potential. www.nya.com

### Seed chair, TumFumi

Following the cradle-to-cradle cycle of sustainability, TumFumi's seed chair is designed to be broken down and buried in the soil once your children have outgrown it. The stool is made of cork chips mixed with flower seeds. Once the chair decomposes into the ground, the seeds germinate and flowers will grow in its place. www.tumfumi.com

### Grey Sparrow Bag kit, Sparrowkids

With the aim of encouraging children to be interested in the environment, all Sparrowkids products are inspired by forms in nature. The Grey Sparrow Bag comes in kit form and is suitable for children aged five and over. A donation from every order is made to the RSPB to protect Britain's sparrow population. www.sparrowkids.co.uk

### Ping Pong printed fabric, Nya Nordiska

Guaranteed to have never been treated with any chemicals and carrying no allergic potential, Ping Pong is a bright, multicoloured printed cotton that has been awarded Oeko-Tex Standard 100 status. www.nya.com

## Sweethome playhouse, A4A Design

A sustainable playhouse for children, A4A Design's Sweethome is made from natural, recycled corrugated cardboard.
www.a4adesign.it

## Find Me playhouse, Rijada

A recycled corrugated cardboard playhouse that can be folded flat and stored, Rijada's Find Me encourages children to be creative through play.
www.rijada.lv

## Teepee, Paperpod Cardboard Creations Ltd

Paperpod's range of environmentally friendly designs are all made from recycled corrugated cardboard. Their factory uses bio-diesel generators and recycles any waste materials used in the production process.
www.paperpod.co.uk

## Play objects, A4A Design

Three-dimensional objects for children to play with, including animals, an apple tree, a prickly pear, a small flower, an aeroplane and a house, are easily assembled from A4A Design's recycled honeycomb cardboard kits. www.a4adesign.it

## Crash Car, Ineke Hans

Crash Car is part of Ineke Hans' 'Black Beauties' series, a collection of 13 traditional products for children. www.inekehans.com

## Dumper Truck, Sam Johnson, Twentytwentyone

Constructed from sustainably sourced wood, Sam Johnson's Dumper Truck forms part of Twentytwentyone's 'Ten' exhibition, which aims to illustrate that sustainable design can be creative, innovative and witty. www.twentytwentyone.com

 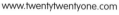

## Wooden Helicopter, Eco Age

Eco Age's Wooden Helicopter is constructed in a fairtrade environment from wood sourced from totally sustainable forests. www.eco-age.com

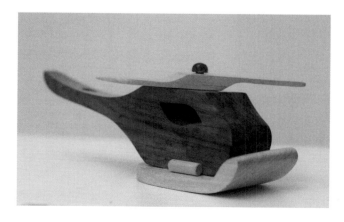

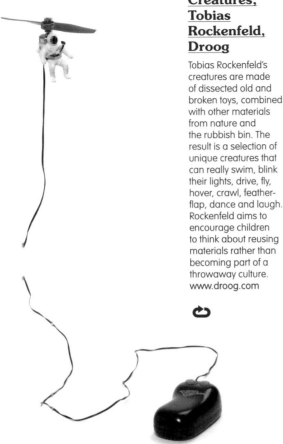

### Creatures, Tobias Rockenfeld, Droog

Tobias Rockenfeld's creatures are made of dissected old and broken toys, combined with other materials from nature and the rubbish bin. The result is a selection of unique creatures that can really swim, blink their lights, drive, fly, hover, crawl, feather-flap, dance and laugh. Rockenfeld aims to encourage children to think about reusing materials rather than becoming part of a throwaway culture. www.droog.com

### Float mobile, Blue Marmalade

With a design inspired by tropical birds and foliage, Float's gentle movement is a joy to watch. The mobile is supplied flat-packed as a kit and is made from polypropylene plastic. Like all Blue Marmalade products, the mobile is made from a single material (even the string between the elements) so it is easy to recycle at the end of its life. www.bluemarmalade.co.uk

### Lucky Fish mobile, Christian Flensted, Flensted Mobiles Ltd

Flensted Mobiles are handmade in Denmark by a family-run business that has been designing mobiles since 1954. Traditional methods and simple raw materials, including recycled cardboard, sustainable wood, wire and thread are used, and employees are local people who work from home, saving on commuting and factory costs. www.danish-design.co.uk

### Owl Bag kit, Sparrowkids

The Owl Bag kit features shapes cut out of scraps of sustainable felt, and is supplied with pre-punched holes, felt flowers and embroidery thread. A donation from every order is made to the RSPB to protect Britain's sparrow population.
www.sparrowkids.co.uk

### Pikos The Hedgehog, The Conran Shop

Pikos The Hedgehog is made with fabric off-cuts that would otherwise be thrown away.
www.conran.com

### The Terrible Twins, Lucy Jane Batchelor

Each of these cute reclaimed tweed and wool characters comes packaged with an adoption certificate and life history. Owners are encouraged to join an online community by registering and sending photos of their new arrivals to the Terrible Twins website.
www.lucyjanebatchelor.me.uk

## Toy Sheep, Eco Age

Eco Age's cuddly Toy Sheep is made from organic wool and natural dyes.
www.eco-age.com

## Reused toys, Muji

It is almost impossible to estimate accurately the precise amount of yarn required to weave a given quantity of fabric. As a result, factories inevitably accumulate a large store of leftover pre-dyed yarn. Muji rescues this yarn to create their collection of Reused products, including a cute collection of toys.
www.mujionline.co.uk

## Doll and baby throw, Fat Rabbit and Purely Hemp Draper's Organic

Hemp is a renewable resource that grows well without artificial pesticides. Renowned for its natural UV-resistance and antibacterial qualities, hemp fabric makes a perfect throw for a baby. This natural hemp baby throw stays cool in the sun and warm when the weather is cool. The rabbit toy is organic inside and out and, with metal-free dyes, is ideal for a new baby.
www.drapersorganiccotton.co.uk

## Make Your Own Monster, Donna Wilson

Made using the leftover scraps from Donna Wilson's knitted textiles, Make Your Own Monster kits include material in pre-stitched creature shapes, stuffing and felt 'bits and bobs' with step-by-step instructions for making your very own unique friend.
www.donnawilson.com

## Sparrow Wall Light, Sparrowkids

Sparrowkids use and source recycled felt and renewable wool and use fairly traded, locally supplied materials. Products such as this felt wall light are designed to remain timeless by using motifs inspired by nature. This in turn encourages children to develop an interest in the environment. The company also donates money from every order to the RSPB.
www.sparrowkids.co.uk

## Soft toys, The Conran Shop

Made from organic cotton and with no hard or detachable parts, these cute bird and duck toys are suitable for newborn babies and children of all ages.
www.conran.com

## Mushrooms, Tamar Mogendorff

All of Tamar Mogendorff's design's are completely unique. The designer uses unwanted scraps of fabrics, carefully hand stitching each piece and ensuring nothing ever goes to waste. www.tmogy.com

## Birdhouses, Tamar Mogendorff

Handmade from scraps of fabric, every piece of Tamar Mogendorff's work is unique. The designer uses vintage linen, wool and mohair as well as silver thread and old ribbons, among other materials. www.tmogy.com

### Office Set,
### Ineke Hans

Office Set is another part of Ineke Hans' 'Black Beauties' series. All items are made of black recycled plastic, which is wind, water, salt and UV resistant, making the products hardwearing and perfect for indoors or outdoors.
www.inekehans.com

### Finish Yourself Junior chair,
### David Graas

By choosing cardboard as the sole material for his Finish Yourself Junior chair, David Graas ensured that it could be easily disassembled and composted at the end of its life. The chair arrives flat-packed in kit form to be assembled at home.
www.davidgraas.com

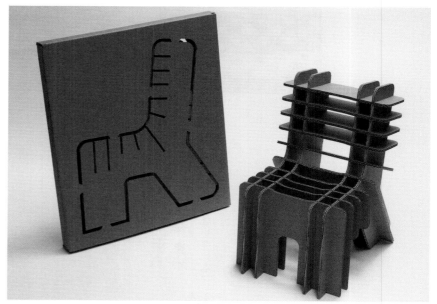

### Toddler Chair,
### Paperpod Cardboard,
### Creations Ltd

The beauty of Paperpod's cardboard furniture, such as this chair, lies in its simplicity – the products are left plain, not only to allow children to be imaginative with decoration, but also to avoid using toxic printing substances.
www.paperpod.co.uk

### Mod Topper tray/table, Lisa Albin Design, Iglooplay

Iglooplay use eco-friendly materials designed to last for many years to come. The Mod Topper tray/table is designed to complement the Mod Rocker (see page 339).
www.iglooplay.co.uk

### Lima Play Table, Lisa Albin Design, Iglooplay

Designed for children aged one year and above, the Lima Play Table has a resource-efficient plywood construction. All the wood is obtained from sustainably certified forests and is available in either a natural, non-toxic finish or painted with water-based paints.
www.iglooplay.co.uk

### Surfin Kids Boogie Board Desk, Inmodern

The Surfin desk is simply and easily constructed from six flat-packed pieces of SmartWood® and is designed to encourage children in independent study.
www.inmodern.net

### Surfin Kids Project Table, Inmodern

The Surfin Project Table can be assembled in minutes with InModern's patented, no-tools assembly method. All Surfin products are made from 100 percent formaldehyde-free FSC certified birch plywood and use eco-friendly, non-toxic, water-based stains and UV cured finishes to minimize greenhouse gases.
www.inmodern.net

## Mini Library, Oeuf

The Oeuf Mini Library is designed at a low height, encouraging children to interact with their own furniture and gain a sense of independence. It is constructed from sustainable birch.
www.oeufnyc.com

## Child's chair, Jasper Start Up

Made from pieces of waste timber, Jasper Start Up's Child's chair demonstrates that sustainable products can be fun and colourful.
www.startupdesign.co.uk

## Linear Bookcase, Inmodern

The simple lines of the Linear Bookcase are constructed from just 12 pieces of SmartWood ®. Sliding doors at the top and bottom provide large areas of concealed storage, while the extra-wide open shelves allow ample room for books, games and toys.
www.inmodern.net

### Mod Rocker,
### Lisa Albin Design,
### Iglooplay

Iglooplay is a children's furniture collection
that combines organic forms, ergonomics
and sustainable materials to playfully engage
children and adults. The Mod Rocker is a rocking
chair constructed from sustainably sourced,
moulded plywood and hardwood veneers.
www.iglooplay.com

### Surfin Kids Art Time Easel,
### Inmodern

Part of Inmodern's 'Ecotots' range, the Art Time
Easel is perfect for budding young artists and
environmentalists. It is constructed from just three
pieces of 100 percent formaldehyde-free, FSC
certified SmartWood® and featuring a durable,
100 percent non-toxic water-based finish. The
easel ships flat to conserve packaging.
www.inmodern.net

### Picket chair,
### Loll Designs

Clean, modern lines are the hallmark of Loll's
'Picket' series, and this junior-sized version is
constructed out of 100 percent post-consumer
recycled plastic (made mostly from plastic milk
bottles). The material requires no maintenance
and is completely weatherproof.
www.lolldesigns.com

### Happy Horse, Ineke Hans

Happy Horse is made from recycled plastic and is part of Ineke Hans' 'Black Beauties' series. The decision to make the products black is partly because most materials come in black, white or natural colours, and also to demonstrate that children do not only react to colours, they also respond to shape, form, texture and ways of playing with things.
www.inekehans.com

### Like-a-Bike cycle, Forest Rolf Merten, Kokua

Like-a-Bike Forest is made using beech plywood obtained from sustainable forestry.
www.likeabike.com

### Croc Rock see-saw, John D. O'Leary, BlueGreen&Co

Part of BlueGreen&Co's Animal Form series, Croc Rock is a self-assembly see-saw that can be used both indoors and out. Made using only FSC certified timber and organic paints and finishes, the charming piece is hardwearing and eco friendly.
www.bluegreenandco.com

### Equus rocking horse, Osian Batyka Williams

This modern rocking horse is constructed from layers of FSC certified plywood profiles pressed together. The holes in the legs allow for extra foot supports to be added.
www.osianbatyka williams.com

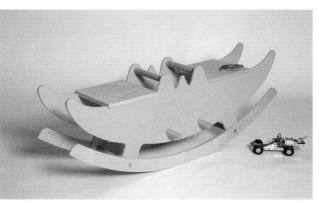

## Toy Fort, Paperpod Cardboard Creations Ltd

An environmentally friendly, cost effective, practical and fun toy design from Paperpod.
www.paperpod.co.uk

### Wooden Blocks Starter Set, HABA

Made using only solvent-free, water-based stains and wood from sustainable sources, HABA was the first German toy-maker to pass the ecological audit and be granted DIN ISO 14001 certification for environmental management. The company actively protects the environment in all phases of production, uses environmentally friendly processing methods and constantly minimizes their use of materials. All wooden waste is used to heat the factory.
www.haba.de

### Barn Blocks, Rijada

Rijada's building blocks are cut from the waste scraps of wood made by a furniture factory. The blocks are sanded and naturally finished with a non-toxic oil to highlight the beauty of the different grains of wood.
www.rijada.lv

### Giddyup rocking stool, Tim Wigmore

Giddyup is a rocking stool made from sustainable materials, with a used leather saddle and gaboon plywood construction. The stool is suitable for children and adults.
www.timwigmore.co.nz

## Woods nursery accessories, Amenity Home

Printed with low-impact dyes in a refreshing palette of chocolate, lime and caramel, these blankets, throws and cushions are designed to introduce children to the joys of nature. Made from a 200 thread-count organic cotton percale, backed with an organic cotton fleece, these accessories are super-soft and cuddly.
www.amenityhome.com

## Nelly Cushion, Claire Nicholson, All Things Original

Claire Nicholson's Nelly Cushion features recycled vintage cotton on the reverse side of the digitally printed elephant design.
www.allthingsoriginal.com

## Yak and Didi rugs, Celia Suzanne Sluijter

Forming part of Celia Suzanne Sluijter's and Janske Megens' XO+ collection of products, these felt rugs are made by women in Nepal under fair trade conditions.
www.xoplus.nl

## Bunnies floor cushions, Amenity Home

Working both as cuddly 'friends' and soft, child-friendly furniture, Amenity Home's floor cushions are printed with eco-friendly, water-based dyes onto either 100 percent hemp or organic cotton fabric. The company also provides eco-friendly cushion insert options, including a high-quality polyester fibre generated from spun recycled plastic bottles, and kapok. Both fillings are encased in an organic cotton cover.
www.amenityhome.com

## Hati cuddle toy, Celia Suzanne Sluijter

Designed by Celia Suzanne Sluijter as part of her XO+ collection, this cuddle toy is made from hand woven cotton by women in Nepal under fairtrade conditions.
www.xoplus.nl

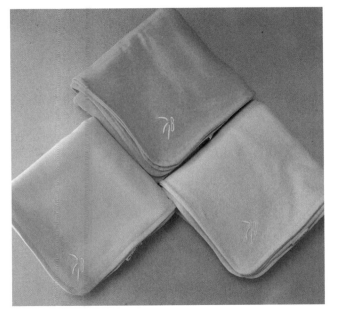

## BambooBaby blankets, Bamboosa

Bamboosa's BambooBaby blankets are made of 70 percent bamboo and 30 percent cotton. They are available in a 'purely natural' fabric option, with no dye on it at all, or coloured pale pink, green or blue, using the lowest-impact dyes possible. Bamboosa avoid using bleach on their products, which is why none of their designs are available in white. They also choose to embroider their logo rather than printing it with ink.
www.bamboosa.com

The author and publisher would like to thank the following institutions and individuals for providing photographic images for use in this book. In all cases, every effort has been made to credit the copyright holders, but should there be any omissions or errors the publisher would be pleased to insert the appropriate acknowledgement in any subsequent edition of this book. Where credit has been given in the caption within the book, it is not repeated here.

21   Table, Pirwi, 2007
41   Subway chair, J. W. Johnson
47   Knit Chair, John Curry, 2004
48   Nendo Cabbage chair, Masayuki Hayashi
56   Natanel Gluska, chair no 44, Xandra Linsin
58   Baley bench, David Manton/Photodrome
62   i b pop chair, Dominic Travers
65   Caught Pouffe, James Champion/
        Evolve photography
67   Weidmann Chair, John Curry, 2005
70   Lisboa upholstered chair, Rita Burmester
81   Studio Aisslinger Gap chair, Steffen Jänicke
81   Bastian easy chair, Michael Sieber
101  SAK bookshelf, Pirwi, 2007
110  Pack of Dogs shelves, Nel, 2007
120  Cog light, Dominic Travers
123  Milk Bottle Light, Marcel Loermans
123  Pegasus reading light, René Bosch
137  Stealth flat-packed floor lamp,
        Magnus Bjerk
139  Arbol Floor Lamp, Dante Dusquets, 2007
160  Cold Vegetable Box and Cold Block,
        Sylvain Deleu
182  Forget-Me-Not Cushions, James
        Champion/Evolve photography
213  Studio Libertiny Honeycomb vase,
        Raoul Kramer
234  Lou Rota plates, Selfridges
254  Catherine Hammerton wallpaper,
        Cho Cho san
258  Piasa, room divider, Pirwi, 2005
282  Watson electricity measuring device,
        Tobu Summerskill
304  Café chair, Fernando Laszlo
304  Transplastic chair, Andrew Garn
306  Treetrunk bench, Marcel Loermans
308  Transrock chair, Fernando Laszlo
321  Full Tank rainwater storage,
        Shannon McGrath

Author's acknowledgements:
Big thanks to Fredrika Lökholm, Peter Richardson, Andrew Wightman and Claire Walsh.